Jones and Bartlett **Self Help Health Guides**

Thyroid Disorders

Warner M. Burch, MD

Professor of Medicine
Division of Endocrinology, Metabolism, and Nutrition
Duke University School of Medicine
Durham, North Carolina

JONES & BARTLETT
LEARNING

World Headquarters
Jones and Bartlett Publishers
40 Tall Pine Drive
Sudbury, MA 01776
978-443-5000
info@jbpub.com
www.jbpub.com

Jones and Bartlett Publishers
Canada
6339 Ormindale Way
Mississauga, Ontario L5V 1J2
CANADA

Jones and Bartlett
Publishers International
Barb House, Barb Mews
London W6 7PA
UK

First Indian Edition 2010
Reprinted 2012

Jones and Bartlett India Pvt. Ltd.
4262/3, Ansari Road, Daryaganj
New Delhi – 110 002
Tel. 011–4361 3900
info@jbpubindia.net
www.jbpubindia.com

ISBN : 978-93-80108-56-8

Printed and bound in India by Raj Press, R-3, Inderpuri, New Delhi - 110 012.

CONTENTS

ACKNOWLEDGMENTS

This is the fifth book I have written about endocrinology, but the first one written for non-medical readers. I am grateful to all the patients I have met, not only for teaching me about disease, but for the opportunity to interact with people. I write this book with great humility, knowing that the "facts" change and that my knowledge is incomplete. I dedicate this book to my patients citing the quote from Reynolds Price, a noted Duke author: "This person, my patient, whatever signs he or she presents, is a human being at least as intelligent and vulnerable as I."

Warner M. Burch, MD

INTRODUCTION

Thyroid diseases are common medical ailments in our society. At least 10 million Americans take some form of thyroid supplementation. One half of the population above the age of fifty years will have thyroid nodules detected by ultrasonography. The incidence of thyroid cancer seems to increase every year. Approximately 330,000 Americans are being monitored for thyroid cancer. The good news for most people who suffer from thyroid disease is that well-accepted treatments are available to enable them to live a normal lifestyle as well as a normal lifespan. This book utilizes a question and answer format to address these conditions. The style is designed for ease of understanding by those who might have a thyroid condition. One of the difficulties in writing such a book is to select appropriate questions to be addressed. The answers may not be directly applicable to any one individual and circumstance because each person is unique. Many of the answers and illustrations have been hammered out through conversations with patients trying to put into practical terms something they can understand about the thyroid. Mrs. Leslie Lobaugh, a thyroid cancer survivor who takes thyroid supplementation to replace what was lost due to surgery, has kindly shared her experience with thyroid cancer and hypothyroidism.

Basic Information

What is the thyroid?

What is thyroid hormone?

What is free T4?

More . . .

1. What is the thyroid?

Thyroid

The glandular structure in the lower neck that makes thyroxine; also, the chemical, thyroxine, may be referred to as thyroid.

The **thyroid** derives its name from the Latin word meaning "shield." It looks like a shield, though it is not a protective structure. The thyroid is located in the anterior lower neck just in front of the wind pipe (trachea). Some would call it a "butterfly-shaped" tissue (**Figure 1**). The normal thyroid consists of two lobes placed lateral to the trachea that are connected by a bridge of tissue just in front of the trachea called the isthmus. On occasion, additional thyroid tissue may be attached to the isthmus, forming the pyramidal lobe. This is a normal variant. Each lobe is about 1.5 to 2 inches (4–5 cm) tall, 0.6 to 0.8 inch (1.5–2 cm) wide, and 0.8 to 1.2 inch (2–3 cm) in thickness. The total weight of the adult thyroid ranges from 0.35 to 0.87 ounce (10 to 25 gm); that's less than ¼ of a hamburger quarter-pounder. The thyroid is quite vascular, having a reddish-brownish

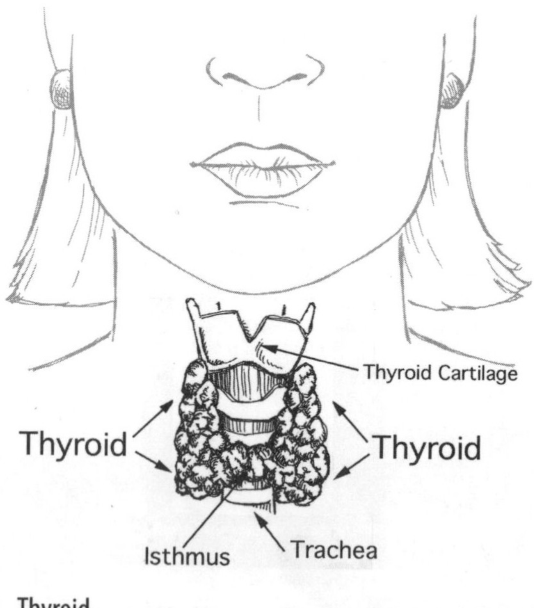

Figure 1 Thyroid.

The thyroid gland, composed of two lobes connected by the isthmus, lies in the front of the lower neck just under the skin. The thyroid rests as a horseshoe structure about the trachea and just below the thyroid cartilage (Adam's apple) which houses the larynx (voice box).

color. Microscopically, the thyroid consists of tiny, hollow microspheres called follicles. Each of these tiny ball-like structures has a central core containing a proteineous material called colloid surrounded by an outer lining of epithelial (follicular) **cells**. Sparsely scattered among the follicles are parafollicular, or C-cells that comprise much less than 0.1% of the total number of thyroid cells. The two types of thyroid cells have different embryonic origins: follicular cells develop from the endodermal pharyngeal pouch and parafollicular cells originate from ectodermal neural crest tissue. This differentiation leads to clinically important distinctions in types of thyroid **cancer**. The thyroid functions as an **endocrine** organ or gland. That is, the thyroid gland produces **hormones** and secretes them into the blood where they circulate and later bind with specific target tissues. The thyroid secretes these hormones: L-thyroxine (T4), L-triiodothyronine (T3), and **calcitonin**. Follicular cells produce T4 and T3, whereas the parafollicular cells make calcitonin.

Cells

Basic elements of tissue; each cell is unique to the tissue of which it is a part.

Cancer

A malignancy that can have several origins.

Endocrine

Dealing glandular secretion of hormones.

Calcitonin

A protein made by the parafollicular or "C" cells of the thyroid; high levels are a marker of medullary thyroid carcinoma.

2. What is thyroid hormone?

Glands such as the thyroid secrete chemical messengers (hormones) into the bloodstream. These messengers circulate to specific target organs and induce a response. For example, the islet cells of the pancreas secrete insulin which travels to the liver and causes the liver to make less glucose, leading to lower blood sugars. The primary chemical produced and secreted by the thyroid is thyroid hormone, levothyroxine or L-thyroxine. Levothyroxine contains four **iodine** molecules leading to the name T4, which is synonymous to thyroxine. The terms levothyroxine, **thyroxine** (T4), and thyroid hormone are often used interchangeably. The thyroid also produces **triiodothyronine**, (T3), which is identical to thyroxine (T4) except for one iodine molecule being clipped off leaving three

Glands such as the thyroid secrete chemical messengers (hormones) into the bloodstream. These messengers circulate to specific target organs and induce a response.

remaining iodine molecules; hence its name, T3. **Figure 2** shows the chemical structure of these hormones. Both T4 and T3 are relatively simple molecules made of two tyrosine molecules along with the attached iodine (which composes about 65% of T4's molecular weight). Both hormones are found throughout the vertebral animal kingdom. Thyroid hormones are the same regardless of the species; T4 is the same in a frog, dog, pig, sheep or cow as in humans. In man, eighty to ninety percent of the thyroid hormone produced and released is T4; the remainder T3. The thyroid also secretes another hormone, calcitonin, in very low amounts, and its significance is discussed in Question 100.

Hormones

Chemicals that are made by glands and released into the circulation, they travel to specific target organs to affect processes; for example, thyroid stimulating hormone is produced by the pituitary and circulates to the thyroid, where the thyroid makes thyroxine.

Iodine

The naturally occurring element (molecular weight 127) necessary for thyroid hormone production.

Thyroxine

Chemical made by the thyroid containing four iodine molecules; also called thyroid, L-thyroxine, levothyroxine, or T4.

Triiodothyronine

An active form of thyroid hormone that contains three iodine molecules instead of four, as in thyroxine; also called T3.

3. What is free T4?

Thyroid hormones circulate bound to binding proteins which act as a reservoir and lead to stable levels of thyroxine. In fact, 99.98% of T4 and 99.8% of T3 is bound. The half-life of T4 is 7–8 days, meaning it takes this

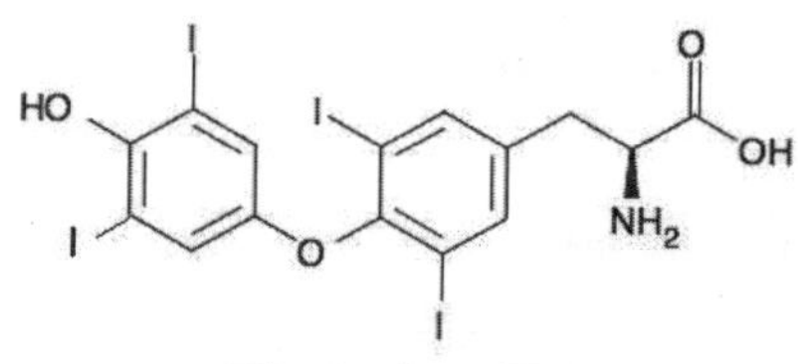

Thyroxine (T4)

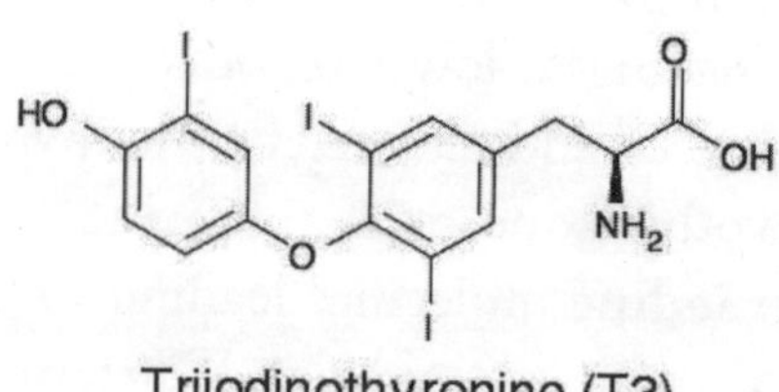

Triiodinothyronine (T3)

Figure 2 Structure of Thyroxine (T4) and Triiodinothyronine (T3).
Both T4 and T3 are relatively simple chemical structures that differ by one molecule of iodine. Thyroxine contains 4 iodide residues and triiodinothyronine, 3 iodine residues.

length of time for the level of T4 to fall from its original value to one-half of its basal level (e.g., 10 μg/dl to 5 μg/dl). The half-life of T3 is about 1 day. Another way of looking at the stability of circulating thyroid is to think of a bathtub full of water as being thyroid hormone. If the drain were just barely opened, it would take 7–8 days for the level in the tub to fall to half full. This observation is critical when withdrawing or replacing thyroxine. It takes 4–6 weeks for any change (addition or reduction) of oral thyroxine dosage to reach a stable level. Circulating levels of T4 are 10 times higher than those of T3. Bound hormone equilibrates with the unbound or "free" T4/T3. **Figure 3** demonstrates the relationship of bound, or total, T4 to free T4 which the equation shifted to the left in favor of bound T4. However, only the free hormones are metabolically active and free to bind with target tissues. Traditional measurements of thyroxine assay the bound or "total" thyroxine because of the abundance of protein-bound thyroxine. Normal levels of serum T4 (bound T4) range from 5 μg/dl to 12 μg/dl. The reference levels of free T4 (unbound T4) depend on the assay, but usually range 0.5 ng/dl to 1.5 ng/dl. That's about 1,000 less free T4 than total T4. It is just easier to quantify a large amount (T4) versus the minute levels of unbound or free T4. Now many labs routinely measure

$$\underset{99.98\,\%}{\text{T4:TBP}} \rightleftharpoons \underset{0.02\,\%}{\text{T4} + \text{TBP}}$$

$$\underset{99.8\,\%}{\text{T3:TBP}} \rightleftharpoons \underset{0.2\,\%}{\text{T3} + \text{TBP}}$$

Figure 3 Equation showing bound T4 vs free T4 and bound T3 vs. free T3. Most, but not all, thyroid circulates bound to serum proteins which act as a reservoir for thyroid hormone. The free hormones, T4 and T3, are the biological active ones.

free T4. Here is an analogy I often use. Picture an ocean (blood stream) where there is a fleet of aircraft carriers (thyroid-binding proteins). On the decks of these carriers are many fighter jets (T4/T3 molecules). These jets sitting on the decks represent the total thyroid level. However, the only jets that count are the few that are in flight patterns about the carriers doing touch-and-goes. Those are the ones free to be dispatched to other places. These jets depict the free T4. Both serum T4 and free T4 reflect the thyroid function. Many drugs and disease processes affect the proteins that bind T4, making it necessary to be cautious in using total T4 as a single test to assess thyroid function. Free T4 determinations avoid some of these pitfalls.

4. What is TSH (thyrotropin)?

The thyroid is the largest endocrine gland. As an endocrine gland, the thyroid produces and secretes hormones, primarily thyroxine (T4) and, to a much lesser extent, triiodothyronine (T3), into the blood stream. These hormones circulate to the target tissues that bind these products and initiate whatever specific role is designated for that hormone. This whole process requires some checks and balances; that is, control mechanisms, to increase or decrease the amount of hormone that circulates. If a gland is allowed to make excessive amounts of hormone, then the effects of the hormone will be greatly accentuated. Likewise, if there is insufficient production of the hormone, then any action that hormone may control will be diminished. A car is a useful analogy. The car needs an accelerator to go and brakes to stop. A heavy foot leads to a runaway car and too much braking leads to a stopped car. The endocrine system is equipped for such increases in speed and has a means of slowing down as well. The thyroid gland does not function autonomously; it is controlled by the hypothalamus and **pituitary** (called the master gland because it regulates other endocrine glands such as adrenal and gonads). The pituitary, a dime-sized structure located at the base of the brain, lies in the midline just behind the eyes. The hypothalamus, which lies just above the pituitary, produces a small peptide called thyrotropin-releasing hormone (TRH) which travels less than a half inch via the blood to the pituitary. In the pituitary, TRH binds to special cells named **thyrotrophs**. The pituitary thyrotrophs make a messenger, **thyrotropin**, also called thyroid stimulating hormone (TSH). TSH circulates to the thyroid gland where it binds onto the follicular cells to control production and release the thyroid hormones, T4 and T3. This is how this system works. The hypothalamus and pituitary gland (specifically the thyrotrophs) sense the levels of T4/T3 in the blood. If the T4 level is lower than what the thyrotroph "thinks" it should be, these cells produce and release TSH into the blood. TSH circulates and binds to its only target tissue, the thyroid follicular cell. TSH stimulates the thyroid to release T4/T3, which raises blood T4/T3 levels. These increases in thyroid hormone are sensed by the pituitary and hypothalamus, leading to an acceptable or "satisfactory" amount of T4/T3. When TSH production slows down, lower levels of TSH are detected by the thyroid, leading to release of less T4/T3. This negative feedback mechanism is classic for endocrine regulation. **Figure 4** shows this cycle.

Pituitary

The master gland located between and behind the eyes that controls the adrenal, thyroid, and sex glands.

The thyroid gland does not function autonomously; it is controlled by the hypothalamus and pituitary (called the master gland because it regulates other endocrine glands such as adrenal and gonads).

Thyrotroph

The pituitary cells that produce TSH.

Thyrotropin

Thyroid stimulating hormone (TSH); a chemical made by the pituitary that causes thyroid hormone secretion.

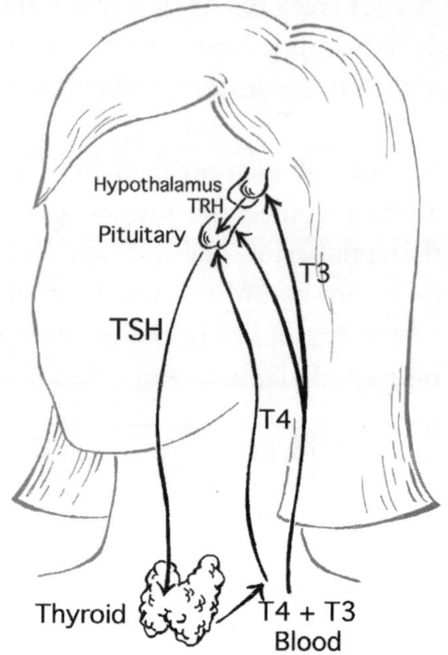

Figure 4 Hypothalamic–Pituitary–Thyroid Axis.

This axis is one of the best known in endocrinology representing classical negative feedback. Circulating levels of T4 and T3 are sensed by the hypothalamus and pituitary. The hypothalamus makes TRH which causes the pituitary to produce TSH which in turn, stimulates the thyroid to synthesized and release T4 and T3. The higher the T4 and T3 blood levels are then sensed by the hypothalamus and pituitary leading to lower TSH levels and in turn, less T4 and T3 production.

5. What is the function of thyroid hormone?

Because T4 and T3 are found throughout many species, one assumes they have basic and significant roles. Trying to describe what the thyroid does is like trying to describe what the foundation of a house does. You know it is important, but you do not recognize how important until the floor moves, the wall cracks, or doors don't shut. Much of what we know about the thyroid's function comes from observation of states in which there is little to no thyroid hormone and from states of excessive amounts of thyroxine. In frogs, thyroxine induces metamorphosis from tadpole to an adult frog, but there is no such change in mammals. The action of thyroid hormone is best noted in the young, where it is critical for growth and development. Neonates and infants need thyroxine for brain and neural development and its absence leads to mental retardation. Similarly, bone and cartilage growth and maturation are stunted, leading to short stature and "failure to thrive." In the young and the adult, thyroid affects **metabolism**, an all inclusive term dealing with the sum of chemical reactions in the living body. In general, thyroxine is necessary for normal protein synthesis and normal oxygen metabolism, often termed metabolic rate. All or any organ system may be affected by excessive amounts of thyroid (**hyperthyroidism**) or inadequate amounts of thyroid (**hypothyroidism**). **Table 1** lists the effects of thyroid on the body's systems.

Metabolism

The process of the sum total of chemical reactions necessary for living things.

Hyperthyroidism

Condition in which too much thyroid hormone circulates, causing a variety of symptoms including increased nervousness, agitation, heart rate, etc.; also thyrotoxicosis or overactive thyroid.

Hypothyroidism

A condition in which less than normal thyroid hormone circulates, causing decreases in metabolic activity that presents in a variety of symptoms including fatigue, depression, cold intolerance, etc.; also known as underactive thyroid.

6. What is the relationship between T4 and TSH?

The levels of T4 and TSH are inversely related. If the thyroid levels are low, the pituitary pumps out more TSH causing the thyroid to make more T4 leading to higher blood T4 which in turn tells the pituitary to decrease TSH secretion. Similarly, if T4 levels are elevated for any reason, the pituitary responds by shutting off TSH secretion, leading to low or suppressed TSH levels in the blood. One can also look at T4/TSH relationship as a see-saw (**Figure 5**): T4 on one side and TSH on the other. However, the fulcrum is not in the center; it is shifted toward the side of T4. What this means is that a small change in T4 creates a large change in TSH (still in the opposite direction). In fact, moving the T4 down by one unit makes TSH go up 100 units. Likewise, if T4 goes up one-fold, TSH

Table 1 Effects of Excessive and Inadequate Amounts of Thyroid Hormone

	Hyperthyroidism (Overactive Thyroid)	**Hypothyroidism (Underactive Thyroid)**
General	Increased appetite Weight loss Heat intolerance	Normal Mild weight gain Cold sensitive Feeling run down
Nervous system	Increased nervousness Sleeplessness Mental competence OK Hand tremors Anxiety	Calmness or indifference Drowsy or sleepy Dull or confused No tremulousness Depression
Circulatory system	Palpitations Fast pulse (tachycardia) Increased blood pressure (usually systolic) No fluid retention	None Slow pulse Hypertension (often diastolic as well) Puffiness and edema
Digestive system	Fast transit of food Frequent bowel movements	Indigestion Constipation
Skin	Warm and smooth skin Increased perspiration Increased nail growth	Cool and dry skin Decreased sweating Brittle nails
Muscular	Weakness (due to muscle loss)	Cramps
Blood	Low cholesterol levels	High cholesterol levels Anemia

goes down one hundred-fold. **Figure 6** depicts this inverse log-linear relationship. For example, raising the serum T4 from 6 μg/dl to 12 μg/dl causes the serum TSH to fall from 3 μU/ml to 0.06 μU/ml. Because changes in TSH are amplified and easy to measure, TSH is used as the first-line measurement in assessing thyroid function.

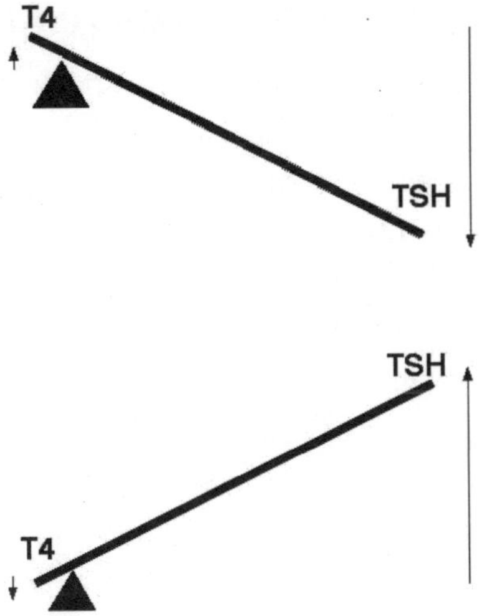

Figure 5 T4/TSH seesaw showing inverse relationship.

As T4 levels rise, TSH levels fall. Similarly, if T4 levels fall, TSH levels rise. Note the fulcrum of this seesaw is very close to T4 which translates into a small change in T4 leads to an exaggerated or amplified change in TSH.

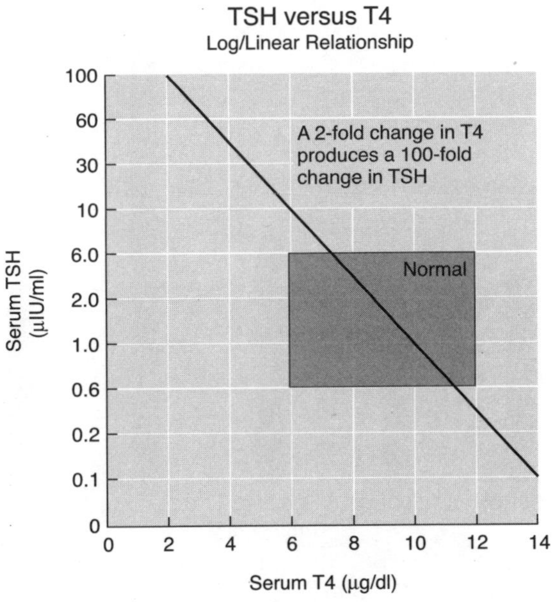

Figure 6 Log-linear relationship of TSH and T4.

This unique seesaw relationship can be expressed mathematically into an equation. A two-fold change in T4 levels leads to a 100-fold change in TSH. For now, serum TSH reflects the most sensitive marker of thyroid function.

7. *What is the normal range for TSH?*

On the surface, this question should have an easy answer. However, the answer is "it depends." It depends on the specific assay, the time of day the blood is drawn, and the range of "normal" established by the lab. The assays for measuring TSH are sensitive and specific and quite reproducible day to day; however, there are slight variations among various tests which lead to minor changes in the normal range. Blood levels of TSH are not static, but vary throughout the day, with the lowest levels in the morning hours and highest levels around midnight. The range can be several-fold within the same individual (for example, 1–2 μU/ml at 8 AM and 5–7 μU/ml at 12 AM). **Figure 7** demonstrates that TSH levels vary depending on what time of day the specimen is collected. The pattern

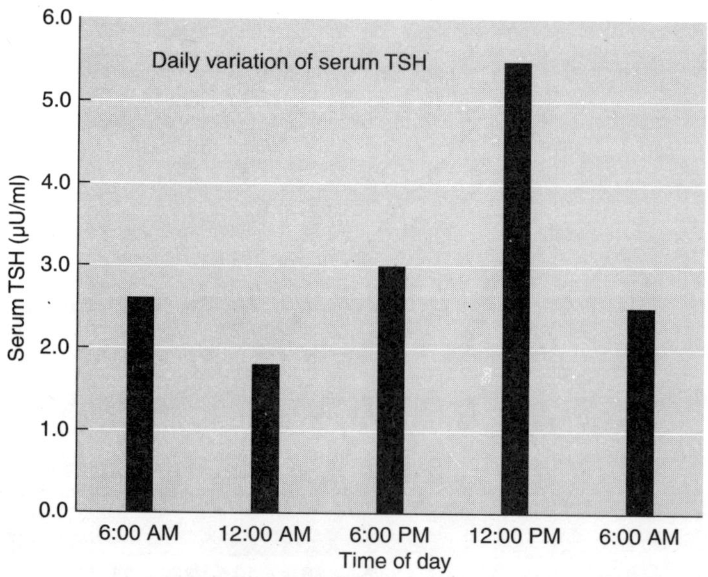

Figure 7 Daily variation of serum TSH.

Serum TSH levels are not static though vary in a tight range. The highest levels are around midnight in those normal sleep habits. This diurnal variation reverses for those who sleep in the day and work through the night. The message of this figure: TSH levels vary during the day.

of diurnal variation changes if someone works the graveyard shift and sleeps during the day (higher TSH in the morning and lower levels in the evening). Finally, most labs establish their normal ranges from blood samples of normal, healthy people who are usually not elderly. For illustrative purposes, let's say 100 volunteers donate blood for TSH determinations and the results are plotted on graph paper. Labs use statistics to define what is "normal." Normal ranges would be set to what is called 95% confidence limits. For TSH assay, the normal range would be 0.5 μU/ml to 4.5 μU/ml. That means 95 healthy volunteers have levels in this range. How about those five healthy people (in theory, 2.5 individuals below 0.5 and 2.5 individuals above 4.5)? They are still healthy but have "abnormal" lab studies. However, their values will be just a little below or above the normal range (for example, 0.3–0.5 μU/ml and 4.5-6.5 μU/ml respectively and not 0.1 or 10 μU/ml). This is an important concept to understand when saying"my numbers are abnormal." Though abnormal from a statistical viewpoint (not in the 95% confidence range), these borderline levels may not necessarily be abnormal for that individual. The best information about TSH levels comes from population studies such as the Third National Health and Nutrition Examination Survey (NHANES III) conducted between 1988 and 1994. HHANES III analyzed thyroid hormone and TSH levels from 13,300 individuals with no known thyroid disease. **Figure 8** depicts their findings. The distribution is not Gaussian (or a bell-shaped curve) but skewed slightly toward higher values. This study showed that the black, non-Hispanic population had slightly lower TSH than Mexican-American and white, non-Hispanic populations. TSH levels do not depend on sex, having the same normal range for men and women. Questions 38 and 72 discuss TSH levels in subclinical hypothyroidism and subclinical hyperthyroidism respectively.

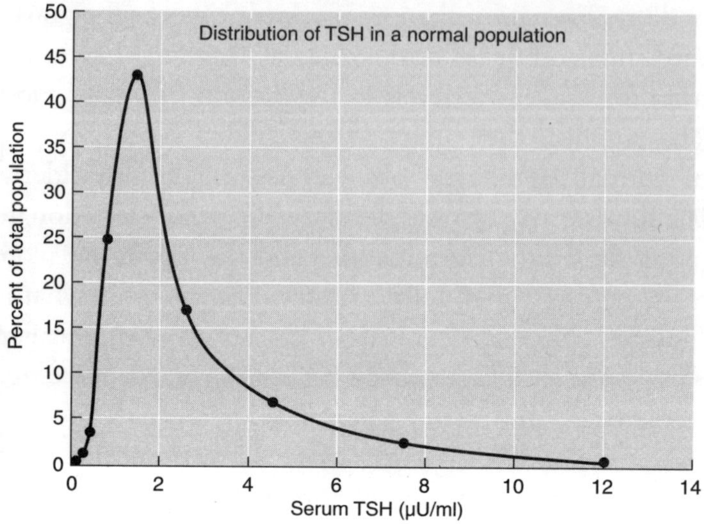

Figure 8 TSH distribution in healthy population from NHANES III study. This graph depicts their findings from data of 13,300 normal individuals with no known thyroid disease.

8. Why is iodine so important?

Iodine, a trace mineral, forms the backbone of thyroid hormones (T4/T3). Each molecule of T4 (levothyroxine) contains 4 atoms of iodine and T3, 3 atoms of iodine (see **Figure 2**). If sufficient iodine is not absorbed by the intestine, then thyroid hormone production decreases, leading to elevated TSH levels. Increased TSH causes a compensatory enlargement of the thyroid (goiter). Finally, the end-consequence of iodine deficiency results in profound hypothyroidism.

Iodine comes from the soil. In mountainous areas and central areas away from oceans where there is little iodine, iodine deficiency causes much suffering and morbidity. Iodine deficiency leads to large goiters in children and adults, hypothyroidism (see Questions 21, 22, and 23), cretinism (mental retardation, short stature, and classic signs of **myxedema** in children—see Question 44), miscarriages, and infant mortality. Developing infants and children are particularly susceptible to iodine deficiency, but supplementation prevents all of these problems. Since the introduction of iodine supplementation to table salt in the 1920s, iodine deficiency has been all but eliminated in the United States. It is estimated that the addition of iodine to salt costs 4 cents a year for each person in the United States. However, 30% of the world's population lives in iodine-deficient areas, meaning that this is a serious global health problem that is totally preventable.

Myxedema

Physical features due to lack of thyroid hormone causing puffy eyelids, facial edema, and fluid retention.

Developing infants and children are particularly susceptible to iodine deficiency, but supplementation prevents all of these problems. Since the introduction of iodine supplementation to table salt in the 1920s, iodine deficiency has been all but eliminated in the United States.

An adult requires about 150 μg of iodine each day to ensure normal thyroid function. Pregnant and nursing mothers need more, 220–290 μg a day. Daily intakes of less than 50 μg of iodine cause iodine deficiency. One-half teaspoon of iodized salt consumed daily sufficiently supplies the physiological requirements for this nutrient. Other dietary sources of iodine include drinking water, seafood (clams, lobster, oysters, sardines and ocean fish) and dairy products from feed additives as well as from disinfectants used on dairy farms. The iodine content of fruits and vegetables depends upon soil content of iodine. Multivitamin preparations may or may not contain iodine. For example, Centrum/Centrum Silver supplies 150 μg of iodine in each tablet. Representative food sources of iodine include regular bread (1 slice), 35 μg; shrimp (3 oz) 30 μg; cottage cheese (2% fat, ½ cup), 50 μg; cheddar cheese (1 oz), 15 μg; haddock (3 oz) 125 μg; ground beef (3 oz) 8 μg; egg (1), 25 μg; and iodized table salt (1 tsp) 267 μg.

9. What is the distinction between the thyroid and parathyroid glands?

Parathyroid glands

Glands located adjacent to the thyroid that control calcium levels in the blood.

The thyroid and **parathyroid** have only two things in common: they share a similar name and both are located in the anterior neck. Sometimes confusion results from their similar names and because the surgical approach leaves an identical scar in the lower anterior neck. This analogy is akin to the eye and ear: they start with the same letter and both are located in close proximity on the head. The embryology and function of these glands is vastly different. The thyroid develops from the floor of the mouth at the base of the tongue and migrates in the midline to rest in the lower neck. The parathyroid glands start as lateral outpouchings (two on each side, sometimes more) of the pharynx and wind up behind the thyroid gland. The thyroid is the largest endocrine gland and the parathyroids are very small; each about the size of a sunflower seed. The name of the parathyroid derives from the anatomy: a structure beside the thyroid. Like the eye and ear, these glands have totally different functions. The thyroid produces thyroid hormones (T4 and T3) to control metabolism, whereas the parathyroid makes parathyroid hormone which manages calcium metabolism. Both glands are subject to increased and decreased function, causing hyperthyroidism/hypothyroidism (high/low serum thyroid levels) and hyperparathyroidism/hypoparathyroidism (high/low serum calcium levels) respectively.

Goiter

An enlarged, and usually visible, thyroid gland presenting as fullness in the anterior lower neck.

Thyromegaly

Thyromegaly is interchangeable with "goiter."

10. My physician found a "goiter" during my annual exam. What is a goiter?

Any enlargement of the thyroid is called a goiter. Medically, the terms **goiter** and **thyromegaly** are interchangeable. The degree of enlargement varies from just barely **palpable** to gross enlargement easily visible from across the room (**Figures 9** and **10**). The thyroid is rarely seen in normal individuals, but it often can be palpated in women with very thin necks. Clinicians use tapes and rulers to assess the size of large goiters. For smaller goiters, thyroid **ultrasound** is helpful, particularly in follow-up, to measure change in size. **Figure 11** shows a tranverse section of a normal thyroid with ultrasound. The trachea is the midline structure; T marks each lobe of the thyroid; C labels both carotids; E shows the esophagus; M denotes muscle; and I indicates the isthmus. This area of the thyroid is easily seen with ultrasound. Reproducible measurements of the thickness of isthmus provide a good marker for size. The normal thyroid isthmus is less 3 mm (0.3 cm) in thickness. **Figure 12** shows a goiter where the isthmus measures 0.92 cm. If the enlarged thyroid

Palpable, palpation

Something that can be felt with the fingertips or the process thereof.

Ultrasound, ultrasonography

A means to identify anatomy of an organ using ultrasound techniques; a valuable aid to follow size but not function of a structure such as a thyroid nodule.

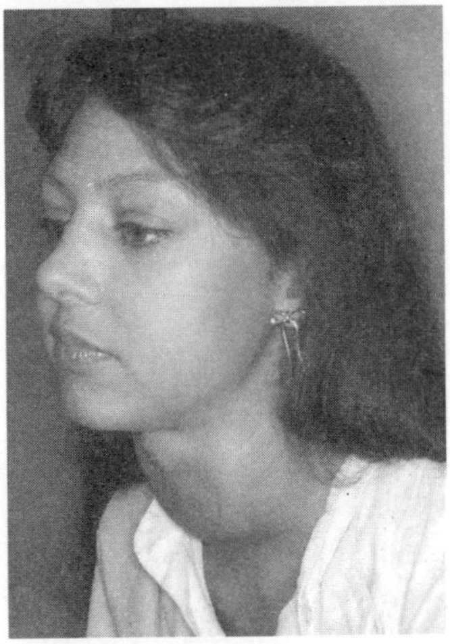

Figure 9 Patient with a diffuse goiter.

The thyroid is generally enlarged three- to four-fold above normal size. This patient had a diffuse toxic goiter.

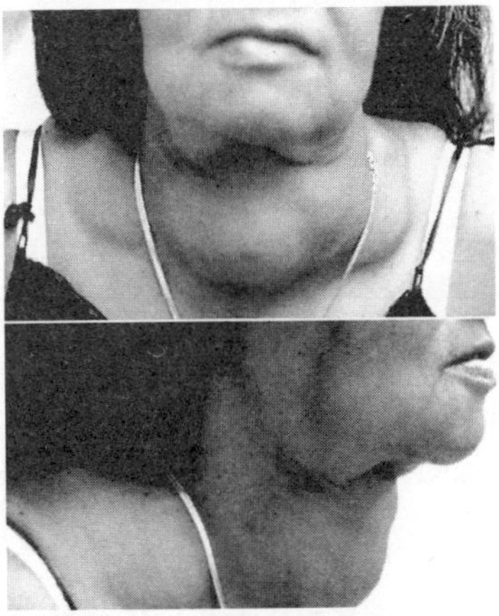

Figure 10 Patient with a nodular goiter. Frontal (upper panel) and Lateral (lower panel) view.

The entire thyroid is enlarged and when palpated had large nodules that merged (similar to a cluster of grapes). Fine needle aspiration biopsy established a diagnosis of papillary thyroid carcinoma.

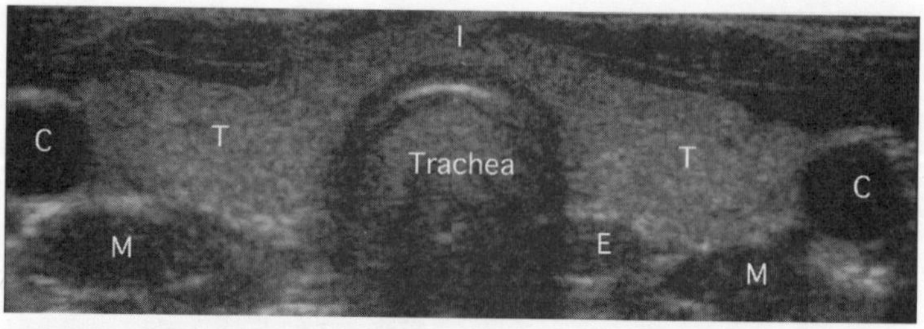

Figure 11 Ultrasound of a normal thyroid.
This is a transverse section of the neck. **T** marks each lobe; **C**, carotid artery; **E**, esophagus; **M**, muscle; and **I**, the isthmus.

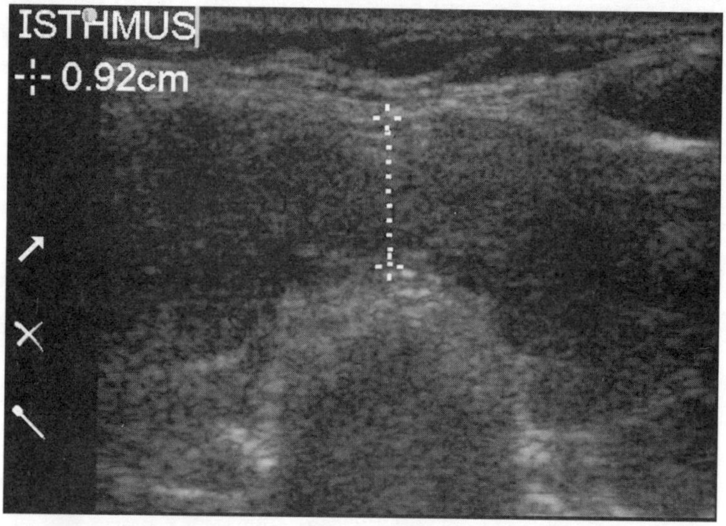

Figure 12 Ultrasound showing large isthmus as part of a goiter.
The normal isthmus measures less than 0.3 cm. This gland also had ultrasound changes consistent with Hashimoto's disease as the cause of the goiter.

grows or extends down into the chest, it is called a substernal goiter. For whatever reason(s), goiters are more common in women (4-fold more likely than men). No racial prediction exists for goiters.

11. What causes a goiter?

There are many causes for a goiter. It helps to start by determining whether the goiter is diffuse or nodular. Any process causing both lobes and isthmus to enlarge leads to a diffuse goiter (see **Figure 9**). A nodular goiter may consist of a single **nodule** (any lump, focal enlargement or discrete fullness that can be seen or palpated (see nodule on left side of **Figure 13**) or multiple nodules (either separate from each other or clustered like a bunch of grapes—see **Figure 10**). Goiters (both diffuse and nodular) may function as a normal thyroid gland (euthyroid or non-toxic goiter), as an overactive or hyperthyroid gland (toxic goiter), or as an underactive gland (hypothyroid goiter). Finally, most goiters are **benign**, but nodular goiters in particular may be cancerous. **Tables 2** and **3** list a classification (and its causes) of goiter.

Nodule

A lump or clump of tissue that forms a mass that may or may not be palpable.

Benign

Not cancerous.

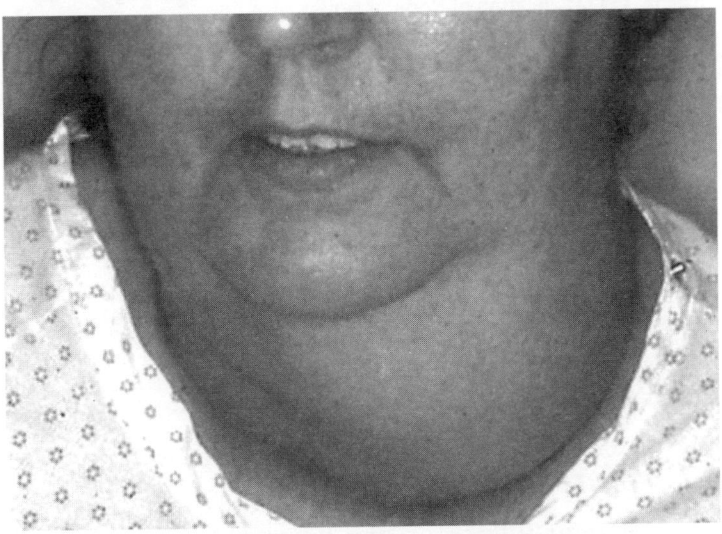

Figure 13 Patient with a single large thyroid nodule on left side. This nodule was benign.

Table 2 Classification of Diffuse Goiter

Non-toxic
Iodine deficiency (world-wide the most common cause—200 million people)
Iodine excess (rare)
Dietary goitrogens (substances that cause goiter include cassava)
Chemical agents (lithium, thiocyanate)
Simple goiter (due to congenital defects in thyroid hormone synthesis)
Any infiltrative disease (Hashimoto's thyroiditis, sarcoidosis, lymphoma)
Hypothyroidism
Toxic (hyperthyroid)
Graves' disease
Subacute thyroiditis

Table 3 Classification of Nodular Goiter

Non-toxic
Thyroid nodule (colloid, hyperplastic nodule, adenoma, carcinoma, lymphoma)
Multinodular goiter
Hashimoto's disease (nodular variant)
Toxic (hyperthyroid)
Thyroid adenoma (Plummer's disease)
Multinodular goiter with autonomous functioning nodules

12. *What is a pseudogoiter?*

The apparent fullness in the lower anterior neck that turns out not to be thyroid is called a pseudogoiter or false goiter. Usually adipose tissue is the culprit here, giving the appearance of a goiter. This can be verified on physical exam by swallowing. Normally, the thyroid moves up with the trachea when one swallows and true goiters, particularly small ones, do the same. If the area in question does not move, then a pseudogoiter is likely. An ultrasound of the neck usually confirms the presence of a normal-sized thyroid. On occasion, a high-lying thyroid or a trachea that protrudes forward mimics a goiter. Rarely, cervical lordosis giving a swan-like configuration of the neck causes a "goiter." Straightening the neck ameliorates the "goiter." This cause of pseudogoiter is labeled Modigliani syndrome (after the long and exaggerated curved neck that distinguished the style of the artist Modigliani).

13. My physician found a mass in the middle of my neck and said it might be a thyroglossal duct cyst. What is a thyroglossal duct cyst and how is it treated?

The thyroid develops in the embryo from an outpouching of the oral tube (pharynx) at the base of the tongue at age of 3 weeks gestation. This nest of tissue moves down in front of the airway as a hollow tube winding up in the lower neck as a bilobed structure at 4 weeks forming the thyroid gland. By the 6th to 7th week, the original tube or stalk atrophies leaving no obvious connection between the pharynx and the thyroid. If this tube fails to totally atrophy, it leaves a remnant that may fill with fluid. This embryonic remnant located in the midline of the anterior neck is called a thyroglossal duct. If the cells that line the original tube start to make fluid, this leads to a noticeable nodule called a thyroglossal duct cyst. When it is low in the neck, the **cyst** can be confused with an enlarged pyramidal lobe of the thyroid. Generally, it is a round or oblong structure which lies just in front of the trachea in the middle of the neck. It usually moves when palpated. Such a nodule can be located from the base of the tongue

Cyst

A fluid-sac that feels like a lump; a cyst may or may not be able to be felt depending on its size and location; cysts are usually benign.

to the lower mid-neck. Though, this mass usually causes no problems, they are generally removed once the diagnosis is established. Thyroglossal duct cysts may become infected, leading to abscess formation. Furthermore, these remnants often harbor thyroid cells that may transform into malignancies. Surgical resection includes removing the obvious nodule and dissecting the tract to the base of the tongue to remove any remnant tissue and generally prevents recurrence. In summary, prophylactic removal of thyroglossal duct cysts prevents the development of abscess and cancer.

14. Following recent bypass surgery for coronary artery disease, I was told that my thyroid tests were abnormal and the doctor suspected I had "euthyroid sick syndrome." What is "euthyroid sick syndrome?"

The levels of thyroxine (T4), triiodothyronine (T3), and thyroid stimulating hormone (TSH) are tightly regulated in health and in sickness. Hospitalized patients often have abnormal levels of these hormones. In fact up to 75% of such patients have values that are out of the reference range. As a response to acute illness, the brain, specifically the hypothalamus, releases much less thyrotropin-releasing factor (TRF), causing the pituitary to decrease its TSH production and release. As a result of less TSH stimulation, the thyroid puts out less T4 and T3, causing lower concentrations of serum T4 and T3 (see Figure 4). In addition, impairment of the normal conversion of T4 to T3 leads to low T3 levels. Remember, 80+% of the circulating T3 comes from T4. The severity of illness correlates directly to the degree of hypothalamic suppression and peripheral conversion blockade of T4 to T3. Minor illnesses produce little to no effect, but major illnesses (severe trauma, burns, pneumonia, major surgery requiring intensive post-op care, etc.) that require hospital admission trigger this response. Some might call this an adaptation to sickness to preserve energy metabolism. This same "sick" response is seen in healthy people during prolonged fasts and caloric restriction. During the first few days following onset of illness, serum thyroid levels fall (T3, T4, and TSH). The low TSH level is in the range of those with mild hyperthyroidism (though not usually less than 0.05 μIU/ml). As one recovers from surgery or illness, the entire process reverses. Measuring TSH then often shows increased levels (usually less than 20 μU/ml) during the recovery stage. Once fully recovered, the thyroid levels return to normal. That is why it is best to recheck these levels four to six weeks following hospital discharge. Measurements of thyroid function studies during hospitalization should be avoided unless there are good clinical reasons to check them. The adaptive response to illness leading to abnormal thyroid levels with return of these levels to normal following illness is called "euthyroid sick syndrome."

15. When are TSH determinations not helpful?

Though quite reliable in establishing primary thyroid disease (hyperthyroidism and hypothyroidism) and reassuring a euthyroid state in normal or thyroid-treated individuals, TSH levels fail miserably in patients with pituitary disease. The pituitary normally senses T4/T3 and responds in a negative feedback manner (low T4-high TSH or high T4-low TSH, see Question 6). For example, patients who have or have had tumors of the pituitary often have low

T4 levels but "normal" TSH. If the pituitary were normal, these individuals should have significantly elevated TSHs. Another situation in which TSH does not accurately reflect the thyroid status is in the euthyroid sick syndrome (see Question 14). TSH levels are modified in acute disease states and following recovery. For these reasons, during hospitalizations may not the best time to measure TSH alone as a check for thyroid status.

Hyperthyroid patients often have suppressed TSH for many months. Following appropriate treatment which restores the T4 to normal, serum TSH may lag behind not rising in a timely fashion. It is not uncommon to see low T4 levels and suppressed TSH in treated hyperthyroid patients. However, after a few weeks TSH levels rise into the hypothyroid range in those patients with low T4 levels. In patients with pituitary disease, serum T4 or free T4 provides the most reliable laboratory marker of thyroid status.

16. I enjoy good health and only take birth control pills, but my physician noted that T3 uptake was low in a recent lab test. What does a low T3 uptake mean?

As noted in Question 3, T4 circulates bound to binding proteins; the predominant binding protein being thyroid-binding globulin (TBG). The bound T4 (or "total" T4) levels range from 5 to 12 μg/dl. Any process that affects the amount of TBG alters the level of total T4. For example, pregnancy or ingestion of oral contraceptives increases

TBG levels, thus increasing total thyroxine levels (both T4 and T3). To interpret thyroid levels accurately, one must know the status of TBG. The T3 uptake study measures the amount of TBG indirectly. TBG has many sites that are capable of binding either T3 or T4. The following sentences describe how this study is performed. First, a tracer amount of radioactive T3 is added to a test tube containing a sample of serum (the fluid that is separated from clotted blood). The radiolabeled T3 tracer saturates all the unbound sites on TBG. Then, a resin (or coated tube containing resin) is added to absorb any unbound radioactive tracer. The serum is separated from the resin, and the resin uptake containing radioactivity counted. The higher level of the TBG, the more of the tracer binds to TBG and consequentially less of the tracer binds to the resin, leading to a low T3 uptake. Likewise, a high resin uptake means fewer sites for the tracer to bind to TBG. This could indicate low TBG levels or more occupied sites of T4/T3 on TBG as seen in excessive amounts of circulating thyroid hormone. The T3 uptake is a "thyroid" test but really has nothing to do with the thyroid or its function; it is an indirect measure of TBG. Similarly, T3 uptake has nothing to do with T3 levels in the blood. It is used as an assessment of TBG status which is necessary to interpret T4/T3 levels. In this healthy female, the low T3 uptake does not mean hypothyroidism, only that she ingests oral contraceptives. A low T3 uptake would also be seen with pregnancy. In both of these situations, the total T4 would be slightly elevated as well because of an increased TBG. To avoid the pitfalls of interpreting total T4 levels, physicians can now order free T4 levels (FT4) that are normal in states that might affect TBG levels.

17. My physician checked my thyroid function studies which showed normal amounts of T4 and TSH. However, the serum contained anti-thyroid antibodies. What is the significance of positive anti-thyroid antibodies?

These antibodies are markers indicating a chronic inflammatory process involving the thyroid (see Question 24). These antibodies are not thought to be pathologic; that is, they do not play a role in the actual inflammatory process. Once tissue injury occurs, products of thyroid cells such as microsomes or **thyroglobulin** are released locally and the lymph system sees these as antigens and produces anti-thyroid antibodies which can be assayed by several methods. Thyroid peroxidase antibodies (TPO), sometimes called anti-microsomal antibodies and anti-thyroglobulin antibodies, are the major anti-thyroid antibodies. Normal individuals may have minute quantities of these in their blood, so labs set limits as to what is positive. Generally, the more vigorous the inflammatory process, the higher the levels (titres) of these antibodies. TPO antibodies are more likely to be elevated than anti-thyroglobulin antibodies. Ninety-seven percent of patients with Hashimoto's disease have significant elevations of TPO antibodies. The presence of TPO antibodies, even with normal TSH, indicates an increased risk for developing overt hypothyroidism, **post-partum thyroiditis** (see Question 71), and miscarriage. For example, women with normal TSH and positive antibodies develop clinical hypothyroidism (low T4 and TSH greater than 10 μU/ml) at a rate of 2.1% per year. This rate increases to 4.3% a year for women with subclinical hypothyroidism (TSH $>$ 4.6 but less than 10) and positive antibodies. Positive thyroid antibodies indicate an ongoing chronic inflammatory process that needs good follow-up with yearly thyroid function studies.

Thyroglobulin

A large protein made only by the thyroid, but which should not be present after the thyroid is missing; used as a marker for persistent or recurrent thyroid carcinoma.

Post-partum thyroiditis

An inflammation of the thyroid following pregnancy that often has three stages (hyperthyroidism, euthyroid, then hypothyroidism); usually transient and without permanent complications.

18. I have been dieting and not lost a pound. It must be my metabolism. So why does the doctor tell me it's not my thyroid when thyroid controls metabolism?

The facts are what they are. You have not lost weight and thyroid controls metabolism. It's the in between and assumptions we make to conclude "something must be wrong with my thyroid" that must be examined. Let's begin with some basic observations. Calories count, but we often don't. If examined closely, one finds that most people underestimate the calories they ingest. In my experience, the number one reason anyone fails to lose weight when dieting is not appropriately assessing the number of calories taken in. Even healthy foods that seemingly have fewer calories trick people. For example, an apple may contain 75 to 200 calories depending on its size. That's a large range and, if applied to other foods, depending how they are prepared, a great source of error in estimating caloric intake. Exercise helps, but in the world of weight loss food calories trump exercise every time. If you walked or ran one mile, that is equivalent to one medium-sized apple in energy. So if you did not eat the apple, that's the same on the energy scale as running a mile. Discouraging isn't it? Our weight and energy balance is tightly controlled. If you ate an extra apple a day for one month (that's not a lot and healthy, too) and you did not walk a mile a day, that translates into almost one pound weight gain in only one month. One pound of fat stores 3,500 calories of energy. Eating an extra apple a day for one year means gaining 12 pounds over that interval. Thyroid hormone controls energy metabolism, but only in a low grade or subtle means. Hypothyroid individuals may be underweight, normal weight, or overweight. Similarly, hyperthyroid patients may be underweight, normal weight, or overweight. Weight in

In my experience, the number one reason anyone fails to lose weight when dieting is not appropriately assessing the number of calories taken in.

either hypothyroid or hyperthyroid individuals depends largely on food intake. Hypothyroid patients gain weight from decreased metabolism only if their caloric intake does not decrease. Hyperthyroid patients may maintain or gain weight with increased food ingestion. If you are old enough to remember when radios had two knobs to control reception: one for coarse control and another for fine tuning, then you will appreciate this analogy. Food/exercise is the coarse control. To find the station, you must use the coarse control. You will rarely find the station with fine control. For sure, although it is definitely easier to lose weight when one is hyperthyroid and gain weight when hypothyroid, it still boils down to calories. If your T4 and TSH are normal, then your pituitary (the tissue most responsive to thyroid in the body) senses the amount of thyroid as normal. Taking extra thyroid to increase metabolism with the hope of losing weight leads to a slippery slope of unhealthy consequences.

19. Following surgery to remove my thyroid, my serum calcium fell. Can you explain what happened?

Hypocalcemia

A condition that might follow thyroid surgery if parathyroid function is compromised.

Hypocalcemia, a low serum calcium that may occur following thyroid or parathyroid surgery, causes a tingling sensation around the mouth, numbness and muscle drawing (contractures) of the hands and feet, and if severe, even seizures. The parathyroid glands are adjacent to the thyroid. Because they (usually 4 glands—two glands on each side) are so small and have a fragile blood supply, they are subject to injury during neck surgery. The parathyroids control the level of serum calcium by secreting parathyroid hormone (PTH) which circulates to the bone where it causes bone to release calcium. The serum calcium rises and feeds back to the parathyroid which senses the level. Once a certain level of calcium is reached, the parathyroid stops releasing parathyroid hormone. If the parathyroid is injured, PTH levels fall and less calcium is released from the bony stores and this leads to hypocalcemia. Often the hypocalcemia is transient for a few days or weeks, if the parathyroid glands are only "bruised" during surgery. Permanent hypoparathyroidism following thyroid surgery is a serious complication requiring lifelong oral calcium and vitamin D supplementation.

20. My thyroidal I-123 uptake was low; so low that no scan was performed. What are the causes for a low uptake?

As discussed in Question 8, the thyroid normally traps iodine. If the thyroid gland does not work, then the trapping mechanism is impaired. Losing thyroid cells as a result of a hypothyroid process such as **Hashimoto's thyroiditis** with end stage obliteration of thyroid cells leads to low uptake. The uptake is therefore low in hypothyroidism. Thyroid imaging is not normally ordered here because the serum TSH is high and the T4 low. The thyroidal iodide uptake is just not as sensitive as these blood studies. If you had other imaging studies with contrast agents within a few weeks, the iodine pool in your body would be high because these agents are iodine-laden. The radioactive uptake of tracer iodine would be low. So a thyroid scan within a few weeks after such procedures is generally useless. If you were hyperthyroid, then a low uptake might be due to a destructive **thyroiditis** (see Question 53) or possibly ingesting too much thyroid hormone. In the latter case, the serum thyroglobulin would be low (see Question 97).

Hashimoto's thyroiditis

An autoimmune state in which the thyroid is destroyed, causing hypothyroidism and often a goiter.

Thyroiditis

An inflammation of the thyroid that may or may not be tender. In the early and acute stages it presents as hyperthyroidism; in the latter or chronic stage with hypothyroidism.

PART TWO

Hypothyroidism

What are some of the facts about hypothyroidism?

What are the symptoms of hypothyroidism (under-active thyroid)?

Are there any signs specific for hypothyroidism?

More . . .

21. What are some of the facts about hypothyroidism?

Among the United States population of around 300 million, at least 10 million Americans are treated for hypothyroidism.

Low thyroid levels or under-active thyroid are synonyms for hypothyroidism. Among the United States population of around 300 million, at least 10 million Americans are treated for hypothyroidism. Hypothyroidism affects women at least 10 times more frequently than men, becoming more frequent as the population ages. For example, there is a ten-fold increase in incidence of hypothyroidism at ages 70–75 compared to individuals age 20–25 (14 individuals/1,000/year versus 1.4 individuals/1,000/year respectively). Subclinical hypothyroidism, defined as mildly elevated TSH (< 10 μU/ml) with normal T4 levels, affects about 8% of the adult female population and 3% of men. A raised TSH and low T4 levels are the laboratory markers for hypothyroidism. However, TSH levels rise well before the serum T4, free T4, or free T3 fall below the normal range. Worldwide, the most common cause of hypothyroidism is iodine deficiency. In the United States and Western Europe, iodine supplementation is universal, so iodine deficiency is uncommon. In these areas, autoimmune thyroid disease (Hashimoto's disease) leads as the most common cause of hypothyroidism, followed by thyroid ablation through radioactive iodine treatment and **thyroidectomy**.

Thyroidectomy

Surgical removal of all (total) or part (subtotal) of the thyroid; removal of either lobe of the thyroid is called lobectomy.

22. What are the symptoms of hypothyroidism (underactive thyroid)?

Hypothyroid patients may have tiredness and fatigue, unexplained weight gain (a few pounds, and that mostly fluid), dry skin, brittle nails, muscle stiffness, joint pain, intolerance to cold, hoarse voice, constipation, menstrual changes, depressed mood, forgetfulness, and trouble concentrating. These are common symptoms that are not specific to thyroid dysfunction. Anyone (healthy or unhealthy) marking off a checklist of these symptoms would find that many would be listed. Many women and men who gain weight easily or cannot lose weight would like to blame an under-active thyroid as the source of that problem. Excessive weight gain rarely relates to hypothyroidism, however. If that were the case, giving thyroid supplementation would likely wipe out the epidemic of obesity in the United States. Because these hypothyroid symptoms are so general, laboratory studies, including T4 and TSH, are necessary to make the diagnosis of hypothyroidism. You may read on the internet (often written by "medical" individuals offering some thyroid product that fixes these symptoms) that blood tests miss the diagnosis of hypothyroidism. These symptoms may improve temporarily with thyroid supplementation. However, long-lasting relief rarely occurs unless biochemical evidence for hypothyroidism exists. Even people with documented hypothyroidism (T4-low, TSH-high) have symptoms that may not go away with adequate thyroid replacement. I interpret these symptoms as not related to the thyroid. For example, if a person tends to be depressed and their physician obtains a TSH of 10 μU/ml (see Question 38), taking thyroid supplementation is appropriate. However, there is no certainty that the depression will improve or go away with T4-treatment. Hypothyroid patients who are obese lose 5–10 pounds relatively easily following treatment by voiding extra retained fluid—those other pounds must be removed the "hard" way (see Question 18). Symptoms that go away or improve dramatically and do not return following thyroid supplementation can be attributed to an under-active thyroid.

23. *Are there any signs specific for hypothyroidism?*

There are some classical signs with profound and long-standing hypothyroidism (myxedema), but health care givers see these only infrequently today because most hypothyroid patients are already treated. Severely hypothyroid patients may exhibit dry, edematous, and flaky skin; puffy eyelids (see **Figure 14**), cool or cold skin; hypothermia (low body temperature); enlarged tongue; pleural and pericardial effusions; ascites (abdominal fluid); lower leg edema (non-pitting; that is, does not leave a hole or depression when pressed); sleep apnea; delayed deep tendon reflexes; carpal tunnel syndrome, and joint effusions. Severe hypothyroidism with these signs of fluid retention is called myxedema. Although none of these is specific to hypothyroidism, a combination of these signs leads to a high probability of that diagnosis. The presence of a goiter with these symptoms would make hypothyroidism quite likely. Fluid retention is also found in heart, liver, or kidney failure independent of the thyroid status. The edema caused by these organ failures often decreases when a diuretic is administered; however, the edema of myxedema fails to respond to diuretics.

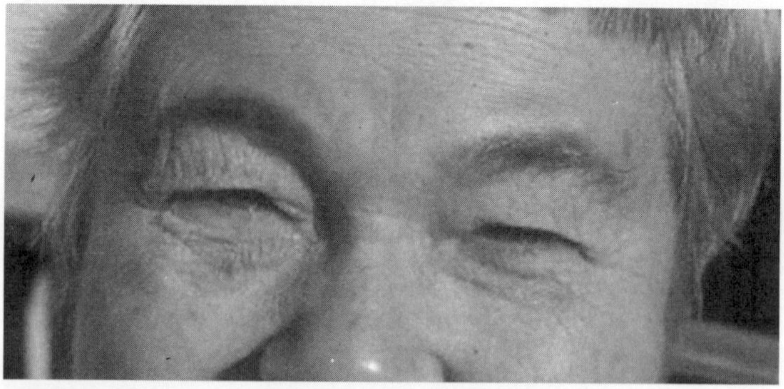

Figure 14 Hypothyroid patient with puffy eyelids.

The edema about the eyes is one of the best findings in hypothyroidism. Other problems include allergy and generalized fluid retention lead to a similar picture.

24. What are the causes of hypothyroidism (underactive thyroid)?

In the United States, autoimmune thyroid disease (also known as Hashimoto's thyroiditis or chronic autoimmune thyroiditis) accounts for most cases of hypothyroidism. It presents as two variants, both associated with lymphocytic destruction of the thyroid follicular cells: goitrous variant (large infiltration of lymphocytes with some fibrosis) and atrophic variant (small thyroid gland with few lymphocytes and much fibrosis). Both variants lead to hypothyroidism associated with elevated levels of anti-thyroid antibodies.

Radioactive iodine treatment of hyperthyroidism is the second most common cause of hypothyroidism (see Question 61). Radiotherapy of the neck for Hodgkin's and non-Hodgkin's lymphoma causes hypothyroidism in 25–50% of these patients. Shielding the thyroid decreases the risk of hypothyroidism.

Radioactive iodine treatment of hyperthyroidism is the second most common cause of hypothyroidism.

Surgery to remove the thyroid for various conditions causes hypothyroidism. In fact, thyroidectomy used to treat thyroid cancer alone affects some 330,000 patients in the United States.

Iodine deficiency is by far the most common cause of hypothyroidism worldwide. Some 29% of the world's population live in regions of iodine deficiency (see Question 8). Less known is the fact that, in some individuals, iodine excess (greater than 1,000 μg/day) causes hypothyroidism by blocking thyroid hormone synthesis. Normally, the thyroid protects itself by escaping from the effect of too much iodine. However, patients with unidentified thyroid disease are particularly susceptible and do not overcome the blockade of excessive iodine, leading to hypothyroidism. This is not a problem for hypothyroid patients already taking levothyroxine. In these treated individuals who have no thyroid, iodine has no effect.

Patients who have or have had pituitary disease or hypothalamic disease may not sense T4 levels because of loss of thyrotrophs and thus do not make TSH to stimulate thyroxine production. This is called central or secondary hypothyroidism.

Congenital hypothyroidism affects about 1 in 4,000 births.

Drugs that commonly affect thyroid hormone synthesis, such as methimazole and propylthiouracil, may cause hypothyroidism in patients treated for hyperthyroidism (see Question 58). Lithium weakly inhibits iodine transport by the thyroid and may cause goiter in up to 50% of patients treated with long-term therapy. Patients who have positive antibodies to the thyroid are particularly susceptible to lithium, causing hypothyroidism in about 20% of such patients, usually in the first couple of years of treatment. Amiodarone, a drug that treats atrial fibrillation, may cause thyroiditis leading to hypothyroidism. In addition, treatment of hepatitis B or C and **malignant** tumors with interferon or interleukin may cause thyroid dysfunction.

Malignant

Cancerous; which may grow rapidly and out of control.

Subacute thyroiditis

Often a painless inflammatory condition leading to transient hyperthyroidism.

Amyloidosis

Abnormal deposits of amyloid protein in many tissues including the thyroid.

Transient hypothyroidism often follows **subacute thyroiditis** (presumably following a viral infection) or postpartum thyroiditis. However, if the insult causes enough thyroid destruction, permanent hypothyroidism might result. On rare occasions, the thyroid may be infiltrated by a systemic disease such as a fibrous form of thyroiditis (not Hashimoto's), progressive systemic sclerosis, or **amyloidosis. Table 4** lists these causes of hypothyroidism.

Congenital hypothyroidism affects about 1 in 4,000 births. See Question 44 for a discussion about this topic.

Table 4 Causes of Hypothyroidism

1. Autoimmune Thyroid Disease (Hashimoto's Thyroiditis)
2. Post Radioactive Iodine (1-131) Ablation/External Beam Irradiation
3. Thyroidectomy
4. Iodine Defidency (Leading Cause World-Wide)
5. Pituitary/Hypothalamic Disease (Central Hypothyroidism)
6. Drugs/Medications—Uncommon
7. Infiltrative/Infectious Diseases—Uncommon

25. My physician tells me I have Hashimoto's thyroiditis as the cause of my goiter, but I do not have any symptoms. Why am I not hypothyroid?

Hashimoto's thyroiditis is an autoimmune disease that focuses on the thyroid. If one looks at an affected thyroid gland under the microscope, many thyroid cells are lost because lymphocytes and other mononuclear cells invade the thyroid, causing a chronic inflammatory response. Literally, normal thyroid follicules are "muscled" out by these inflammatory cells. For most individuals, hypothyroidism develops slowly over many months to years. The very first stage begins with loss of thyroid follicular cells. If enough thyroid cells are lost, then T4 levels fall and, as a consequence, TSH levels rise in an attempt to keep the remaining thyroid cells functioning at full pace. Once about 80% of the thyroid is lost, the TSH remains persistently elevated. Our bodies have organs that function quite well until a critical mass is reached. We call that reserve. Once below this reserve, abnormal studies indicate poor function. For example, if you have two healthy kidneys, you can donate one and still have normal renal function. You can lose 80% of your pancreas and still have normal pancreatic function. The same can be said of the thyroid because of its great reserve. As long as 20% of the gland functions normally, then blood studies of the thyroid remain within the reference or normal range. If one loses enough thyroid cells, however, thyroxine (T4) production decreases and this is followed by an immediate response in TSH secretion to stimulate the thyroid to produce T4. If the serum T4 does not rise in response to TSH stimulation, the pituitary continues to put out more TSH ("hitting and beating" the thyroid), raising TSH levels even higher in attempts to normalize T4 levels. Remember, the relationship between TSH and T4 is a log-linear one, in that a small change in T4 leads to a great change in TSH (see **Figure 6**). This condition describes the biochemical changes of subclinical hypothyroidism. As the TSH levels increase, the thyroid responds by preferentially secreting more T3 than normal (by converting more T4 to T3 within the thyroid). In addition, the conversion rate of T4 to T3 in the brain increases in attempts to restrict the impact of thyroid hormone deficiency. This explains why serum T3 levels are mildly elevated or normal early in the course of hypothyroidism when serum T4/free T4 levels are low and TSH levels are high. As the hypothyroid state progresses with further falling of T4 levels, T3 levels decrease to below normal as well. Even though you may have a goiter due to Hashimoto's thyroiditis, there is still enough thyroid functioning to give you normal thyroid levels and for you not to be hypothyroid. However, one would predict that with time (months to years) you would develop low thyroid levels as the disease progresses. That's good enough reason to have annual check-ups or more frequent follow-up should you develop hypothyroid symptoms.

26. Since the diagnosis of hypothyroidism rests on the TSH level, what is upper limit of normal for TSH?

Establishing that a TSH is above normal level has significant clinical importance because the diagnosis of hypothyroidism is usually made based on this value. Hypothyroidism commits the individual to lifelong thyroid replacement or supplementation. Again, the question is what is normal. TSH levels range over a spectrum, so where does one draw a line and say this TSH is low or high? That question has been addressed by many **endocrinologists**. Let's look at some observations using the results of NHANES III study (**Figure 8**). The median TSH was 1.39 μU/ml; that is, one-half of the population had values below 1.39 and one-half had levels above 1.39. Ninety-seven and half percent of these normal individuals had levels less than 4.12 μU/ml. Realizing that a few normal individuals will have levels above 4.1 μU/ml and still be "normal" (see Question 7), many endocrinologists use a level above 4.5 μU/ml as the upper limit of normal. Other endocrinologists have "lowered the bar," saying that patients with TSH above 2.5 μU/ml should be treated. If that were the case, about 12% of the normal adult U.S. population (translated > 20 million) with levels between 2.5 and 4.5 μU/ml would be on thyroid supplementation. If such criteria were used, many people without thyroid disease would be treated unnecessarily and run the risks of overexposure to thyroid hormone.

Endocrinologist

A physician who specializes in the diagnosis and treatment of endocrine disorders.

27. What is the treatment for hypothyroidism?

Ten million people in the United States currently take thyroid hormone supplements, primarily to treat hypothyroidism.

The first hypothyroid patient was prescribed sheep thyroid, "minced, lightly fried, to be taken with currant jelly once a week." Soon thereafter, in 1895, a pharmaceutical company produced desiccated animal thyroid, which was the mainstay therapy for 70 years. In the early 1970s, synthetic levothyroxine (T4) and tri-iodothyronine (T3) started to be used. Because treatment with T4 alone enables the body to generate T3 as needed, levothyroxine is most physicians' current choice for thyroid replacement. Ten million people in the United States currently take thyroid hormone supplements, primarily to treat hypothyroidism. Levothyroxine is identical to the hormone missing in hypothyroid patients. It is easy to take (once a day by mouth) and leads to thyroid levels comparable to those of individuals with normal thyroid function. In 2005, the brand name levothyroxine, Synthroid, was the second most prescribed drug in the United States (Lipitor was #1), though the company's sales revenue ranked #62. This means it is a relatively inexpensive medication. The treatment must be lifelong. Failure to take thyroid preparation is the leading cause of symptom recurrence. Hypothyroid patients commonly relapse because they run out of medication, forget to refill their prescriptions, and then overlook the often insidious return of symptoms. Very rarely is hypothyroidism transient (usually due to medication), so the need for permanent replacement therapy should be indelibly ingrained into you, the patient, and your family. **Figure 15** depicts the dramatic effect of a few weeks of levothyroxine replacement. The upper panel shows classical facial edema (myxedema facies) when the patient presented to the clinic. I asked her to stick out her tongue, and it was mildly enlarged as well. The

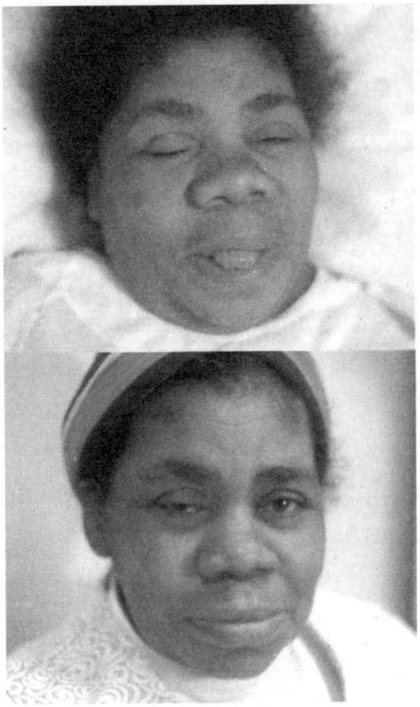

Figure 15
Hypothyroid patient at presentation (upper panel) and after receiving levothyroxine for six weeks (lower panel).

Treatment of documented hypothyroidism leads to some dramatic physical changes.

lower panel shows the same patient 6 weeks later, after taking oral T4, demonstrating the resolution of the fluid retention with levothyroxine alone.

28. What's the cost of thyroid replacement therapy?

Levothyroxine is relatively inexpensive. The cost varies depending on brand, dosage, drug plan and amount of copayment. In the United States, if you use 0.1 mg of levothyroxine each day and purchase 100 tablets, the daily cost breaks down as follows: Synthroid, 52 cents; Levoxyl, 37 cents; Levothroid, 26 cents; and levothyroxine, 29 cents. Desiccated thyroid (Armour) costs 25 cents a day for 60-mg tablets. Taking Cytomel 5 μg twice a day increases the daily cost by an additional $1.46.

29. I am being treated for hypothyroidism. Should I take brand name or generic levothyroxine?

For years, Synthroid has been the most-used levothyroxine in the United States and it still has the highest market share (62%) of levothyroxine sold. Other levothyroid brands include Levoxyl, Levothroid, and Unithroid. All have FDA approval. Physician preference for prescribing any one brand often relates to habits and interaction with professional societies, continuing education programs, and pharmaceutical representatives as well as cost. Some people prefer Fords; others, Chevys; still others, Toyotas, etc. All are automobiles that get from point A to point B. That's pretty much how it has been with thyroxine replacement therapy using brand name levothyroxine. In recent years, the FDA has approved generic levothyroxine, stating that these preparations are bioequivalent by meeting the standards set for branded levothyroxine. Much debate among experts concentrates on defining bioequivalence and testing to measure bioequivalence. Drug plans and formularies push generic levothyroid because it is less expensive. Pharmacists in many states can substitute generic levothyroxine, usually without the necessity to inform the prescribing physician or healthcare provider. There are reasons for concern. Although each tablet now contains a comparable amount of T4 as assayed by chromatography, the actual packaging of the T4 varies by manufacturer. For example, the size of 0.1 mg of levothyroxine is smaller than a grain of sand. To deliver this minute particle, the levothyroxine has to be packaged in a tablet that contains buffers and additives to assure stability and solubility. That means most of the ingested tablet is not levothyroxine. How well one absorbs the levothyroxine may vary with each product. For most people, generic levothyroxine works quite well. However, since manufacturers of generics use different additives to package the levothyroxine, the absorption of T4 may vary when switching from one drug company to another. The safest route is to stay with the same name brand drug you have been taking. If cost and drug plan preference are factors, then use generic levothyroxine. If you change preparations, be sure to have your thyroid function tested 5–6 weeks after starting different levothyroxine, particularly if you feel any change in your health.

30. I have had hypothyroidism for several years and have been treated with levothyroxine. I've heard about natural thyroid. What is "natural" thyroid?

All mammals make and store thyroid hormone in their thyroid glands. The human thyroid acts as a reservoir for about 100 days' supply of thyroxine. For over a hundred years, animal thyroid glands have been used effectively to treat hypothyroid patients. Thyroid glands from cows, pigs, and sheep have been processed, dried, ground, and packaged by weight into tablets. For years, "Armour" thyroid has been the premier brand of desiccated thyroid among available brands that include "Armour" thyroid, Westhroid, Naturethroid, and Bio-throid; most use porcine thyroids as their desiccated thyroid source. The ratios of T4 to T3 vary among species. For example, desiccated porcine thyroid contains both T4 and T3, but at a molar ratio (T4/T3 :: 4.2/1) different from human thyroid (T4/T3 :: 14/1). All you need do to determine whether you are taking natural thyroid is open the pill bottle and sniff. If it stinks, then you have "natural" thyroid. When referring to use of desiccated thyroid for thyroid hormone replacement, it is often said that "natural thyroid is natural only to pigs and not to humans."

31. If T3 is the more biological active thyroid hormone, why not use it to treat hypothyroidism?

T3, in the form of Cytomel, can be administered orally and has been used to treat hypothyroidism. Cytomel works quite well; however, that being said, here are the reasons why it is not generally prescribed. Once taken, the Cytomel is rapidly absorbed, with blood levels of T3 peaking within a couple of hours. **Figure 16** shows the levels of free T3 in three different individuals after taking 25 μg of Cytomel orally. Serum free T3 levels peak around 2 hours, rising 4-fold above the starting level. By four hours later, serum free T3 levels are still above baseline values by some two-fold, reaching their nadir by 12 hours. In order to supply adequate T3 to the body, hypothyroid patients need to take Cytomel

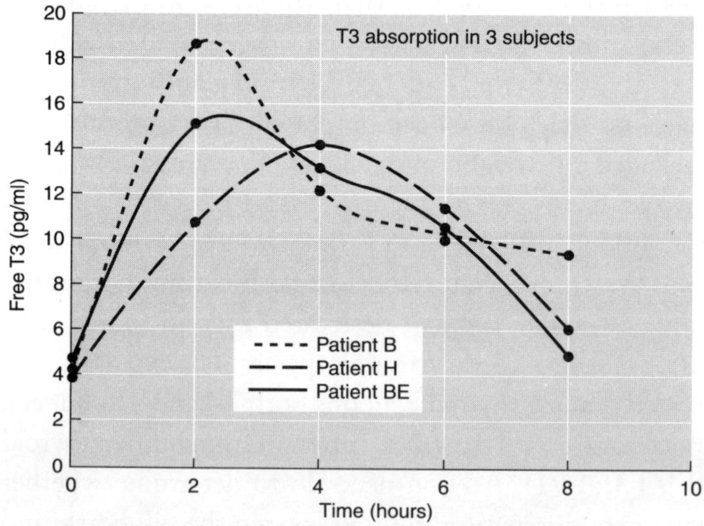

Figure 16 Serum levels of T3 levels after taking Cytomel (T3) orally. Three normal individuals start with a baseline serum T3 around 4 pg/ml, take T3, and then have serum T3 determinations. Note the large 3–4 fold increase in serum T3 that lasts for several hours.

at least two to three times a day. A lifelong medication that needs to be taken three times a day is just not convenient. Also, the cost of Cytomel is 3–4 times that of branded levothyroxine. However, the major drawback of oral T3 is that it does not mimic normal thyroid physiology. Normal blood levels of T3 are quite stable and about 1⁄10 of those of T4. There are no spikes of T3—just a persistent smooth amount of T3 circulating in contrast to the levels seen in Figure 16 where serum T3 levels rise acutely and stay elevated for several hours. Most side effects of Cytomel relate to these non-physiological levels of T3 which may raise heart rate, precipitate palpitations, cause tremors, and increase nervousness and anxiety. In the elderly, T3 may initiate atrial arrhythmias and atrial fibrillation. Because of its short half-life, some physicians use Cytomel temporarily while withdrawing levothyroxine for body scanning in follow-up of thyroid cancer patients. The advantages of levothyroxine trump T3 in almost every situation.

32. I have been on levothyroxine (sodium) to treat my hypothyroidism, yet still am tired. How about adding T3 (Cytomel) to my regimen?

The potential benefits of combinations of both T4 and T3 have been exalted for many years. The idea was that T4 alone might not provide enough T3 because conversion of T4 to T3 in the body might be impaired. Since T3 is metabolically more active than T4, taking additional T3 should help symptoms. In 1999, an article in the New England Journal of Medicine (NEJM 340:424-429) caught the eye of all whose symptoms were not relieved by taking levothyroxine. These authors found that patients treated with both T4 and T3 for five weeks had improved mood and neuropsychologic function compared to patients treated with T4 alone. This landmark study seemed to answer the question of using combination T4 and T3. However, there has been one major problem: these results have not been replicated. Nine subsequent studies failed to show significant benefits when using combined therapy. One explanation for the positive effects of the NEJM article is that these patients were overtreated with T4/T3 because 20% of patients had suppressed TSH (indicating subclinical hyperthyroidism). In fact, the at rest pulse rate in patients treated with T4 and T3 increased significantly. For years, the benefits of subclinical hyperthyroidism on mood have been used by psychiatrists to enhance the effects of antidepressant drugs. I tell my patients: "Running on high test gasoline going down the interstate at 80 MPH is nice, but not normal." No doubt some patients respond better to combined T4/T3 therapy, but it is not predictable, uniform, nor long-lasting. The placebo effect is real and must be remembered by all who embark on this course. Every individual who considers combined therapy (levothyroxine and T3 or desiccated thyroid—see Question 33) should know it is not the panacea for thyroid hormone replacement.

33. *Are there thyroid replacement medications other than levothyroxine?*

More than ninety-five percent of hypothyroid-treated people do well with levothyroxine. The remaining few percent of patients who remain symptomatic despite having normal thyroid studies desire to feel better and ask if there is something else to take. There is no good answer as to why they remain symptomatic. A logical answer seems to be that there must be something missing or something not replaced. Since T3 is not found in levothyroxine tablets but is found in desiccated thyroid (Armour thyroid or Westhroid), Thyrolar (combination of T4/T3), or in using levothyroxine with T3 (Cytomel), why not use a preparation that contains both T4 and T3? You could take desiccated thyroid, Thyrolar, or T4 with Cytomel. These combinations treat hypothyroidism quite well and have been used for years. That has been the approach to treating patients who remain symptomatic. Many who are started on these T4/T3 preparations feel better for a few weeks and then experience a return of their symptoms; others feel no difference; and still a few others, are much improved. Testimonials about the virtues of the combination therapy abound, but predicting who will do well requires a Ouija board. Systematic studies have not proved that alternative thyroid preparations are better than levothyroxine alone. If one weighs the pros and cons of levothyroxine alone compared to T4/T3 combinations, levothyroxine wins hands down. Stable blood levels of both T4 and T3 that mimic levels of individuals with normal thyroid function is the major suit for levothyroxine alone. Patients who take T3-containing preparations have levels of T3 far above normal shortly after taking the tablet (**Figure 16**). This is not normal physiology where serum T3 concentrations are level and quite stable. Such unnatural peaks may cause tachycardia and tremors and precipitate atrial arrhythmias, particularly in the elderly. Levothyroxine touts once-a-day dosing, cost-effectiveness, and widespread availability. Stability and shelf-life are generally better than T3 combinations. For example, the manufacturer of Thyrolar recommends refrigeration of their product.

34. I have been treated for hypothyroidism. How often should I have my thyroid levels checked?

Once the diagnosis of hypothyroidism is established and levothyroxine begun, you should have your thyroid levels checked in 6–8 weeks. After your thyroid levels (TSH, T4) are normal, then follow-up visits every 6–12 months are all that are needed. The reason is that a normal thyroid gland makes a fixed amount of T4 each day. If someone who has no thyroid tissue takes a fixed amount of levothyroxine a day equivalent to what a normal gland produces, the level of thyroxine will be quite stable. If your levothyroxine dose requires a change, you should have repeat studies every 6-8 weeks until your thyroid levels are normal. If you are being treated for thyroid cancer, more frequent checks may be necessary for the first year. If you are symptomatic or have a change in brand and type of levothyroxine, then having these thyroid studies is important. For most patients who take their levothyroxine consistently, once a year follow-up with their physician works well.

35. What is the optimal TSH for patients treated for hypothyroidism?

What we know about TSH is that each healthy person's mean TSH remains relatively fixed within the normal range (0.4 to 4.5 μU/ml). If TSH is measured monthly under the same conditions, some individuals maintain a mean TSH in the "low" range of normal (e.g., 0.6–1.2 μU/ml) and some in the "high" end of normal (e.g., 2.5-4.0 μU/ml). Since no one really ever knows their mean TSH prior to development of hypothyroidism, physicians must treat the hypothyroidism to "normalize" the TSH level.

Because 86% of the normal population has TSH between 0.4–2.5 μU/ml (see **Figure 8**), this seems to be a reasonable goal for levothyroxine-treated hypothyroid patients.

36. What medications or over-the-counter remedies should I avoid while taking levothyroxine (T4)?

If your thyroid function studies (TSH and T4) are normal, you can take the same medications as a person who is not taking thyroxine. You would be considered euthyroid. There are, however, medications that you should not take at the same time as ingesting levothyroxine. Iron tablets or multivitamins that contain iron should not be taken together with levothyroxine because iron and T4 bind as a complex and neither is absorbed as well as when taken separately. Allow at least a couple of hours between taking T4 and iron. Calcium tablets, bile salt binders (cholestyramine), aluminum-containing antacids, stomach-coating meds (sucralfate), and soy (formulas and protein cocktails) need to be spaced apart from levothyroxine as well. A practical solution is to take levothyroxine at bedtime on an empty stomach and any other medications in the morning or throughout the day. Alternatively, one could take T4 first thing in the morning and wait to take medications. It is best not to take T4 with food, even though many people can take food and T4 together without any compromise in absorption. If there is any suggestion of fluctuating thyroxine levels, then make sure T4 is taken separately from any food or medications. Your doctor is well aware that certain drugs, such as Phenobarbital and Dilantin, affect the metabolism of thyroxine. Again, as long as you are euthyroid, you need not worry about taking other medications such as cold remedies and decongestants. If uncertain about any medication, ask your physician.

37. I have been prescribed levothyroxine to treat hypothyroidism. I have missed taking some tablets. What should I do?

Once-a-day dosing of thyroxine works well because of its prolonged half-life. Picture the level of T4 in the blood as a bathtub full of water. If you stop taking T4 (levothyroxine) by mouth, it will take 7 days for the level of T4 to fall to half full. This means missing one or two days has minimal effect on circulating T4 levels. However, if levothyroxine is not taken consistently on a daily basis, the level of T4 will be less than expected. If you miss one day, you can take an extra tablet the next day without harm. Since the treatment of hypothyroidism is lifelong, you should get into a daily habit of taking the levothyroxine.

38. I have been told that I have subclinical hypothyroidism, but I do not have any definite symptoms. What is subclinical hypothyroidism?

Vague and non-specific symptoms of hypothyroidism alone do not merit a diagnosis of subclinical hypothyroidism because these symptoms occur with the same frequency among individuals with TSH levels in the normal range.

Subclinical hypothyroidism is similar to subclinical hyperthyroidism in that it is a laboratory diagnosis. The diagnosis of subclinical or mild hypothyroidism rests on the finding of an elevated serum TSH above the reference range (0.4–4.6 μU/ml). Vague and non-specific symptoms of hypothyroidism alone do not merit a diagnosis of subclinical hypothyroidism because these symptoms occur with the same frequency among individuals with TSH levels in the normal range. The biochemical features include normal levels of T4, free T4, and T3 associated with serum TSH between 4.6 and 10 μU/ml. Defining the upper limit of normal is somewhat controversial (see Question 7). Persistent TSH levels (above 10 μU/ml) confirm the diagnosis of overt hypothyroidism. In this condition, serum T4 concentrations are below the normal reference range or at the very lower limits of normal compared to normal T4 levels in subclinical hypothyroidism. The three most common causes of subclinical hypothyroidism in order of frequency are as follows: patients with autoimmune thyroid disease (Hashimoto's thyroiditis), patients who have been treated for hyperthyroidism usually with **I-131**, and patients with documented hypothyroidism including surgical hypothyroidism who fail to take their thyroxine or who need an increase in their dose of thyroxine. Other causes of elevated TSH include the recovery phase of euthyroid sick syndrome (see Question 14), resolving subacute thyroiditis (see Question 53), untreated adrenal insufficiency, and laboratory or clerical error. These borderline TSH levels should be retested prior to considering any long term therapy. Patients with subclinical hypothyroidism are typically asymptomatic, but the symptoms characteristic of hypothyroidism overlap the complaints of the general population in such similarity that it is almost impossible to tell what might be related to the thyroid and what is not (see Question 22).

I-131
The radioactive isotope of iodine that emits radiation used to treat hyperthyroidism and well-differentiated thyroid carcinoma.

39. How common is subclinical hypothyroidism?

Any large screening program identifies individuals with "abnormal" lab studies that may or may not be related to some clinical condition. This is true with subclinical hypothyroidism in which the T4, T3, free T4, and free T3 are within the normal reference range but the TSH is just above normal, ranging from 5 to 10 μU/ml. Using more sensitive TSH assays identifies up to 4% of the general population with subclinical hypothyroidism, with an even higher frequency in the elderly. Ten to twenty percent of women and 5–10% of men over 65 years have elevated TSH levels. Subclinical hypothyroidism occurs about five times more frequently than subclinical hyperthyroidism. Numerous studies fail to show any increase in mortality with subclinical hypothyroidism. Biochemical studies looking specifically for increased cholesterol levels as seen in overt hypothyroidism have not been revealing. What we do know is that patients who have thyroid peroxidase antibodies (TPO) are more likely to progress to overt hypothyroidism in which the TSH is greater than 10 μU/ml and T4 levels are low. We also know that individuals who have subclinical hypothyroidism are more likely to progress to overt hypothyroidism than are individuals with normal TSH levels. Women with subclinical hypothyroidism and positive TPO antibodies develop overt hypothyroidism at a rate of 4.5% per year. Women with subclinical hypothyroidism who do not have TPO antibodies progress to overt hypothyroidism at a rate of 2.5% year. Before anyone bets for sure that you're going to progress to overt hypothyroidism, you should know that follow up studies involving subjects with subclinical hypothyroidism show that over a four-year interval, 20–30% of these individuals experience a return of their TSH to the normal range without any treatment.

40. When should subclinical hypothyroidism be treated?

This is not an easy question to answer. Much depends on the individual and the health care provider who knows each individual circumstance. Here are some guidelines for considering thyroid supplementation in subclinical hypothyroidism. Patients who have a goiter and positive thyroid antibodies are usually started on thyroxine. In this situation, the likelihood of developing overt hypothyroidism is high and taking thyroxine prevents clinical hypothyroidism. Younger patients with positive TPO antibodies, pregnant women or women anticipating pregnancy who have elevated TSH, and patients who have had I-131 to treat hyperthyroidism are all reasonable candidates for thyroid supplementation. Older individuals with subclinical hypothyroidism are best observed. But what about the weak and tired individual with a TSH of 6.7 μU/ml who wants something done because nothing else was found? This is not an uncommon scenario. Several studies have failed to demonstrate any consistent relief of symptoms with thyroid supplementation or any change in biochemical parameters such as LDL-cholesterol, unless the TSH was greater than 10 μU/ml. A therapeutic trial (to see if thyroxine helps with the symptoms) is worth the try. If symptoms persist after taking medication for several months, thyroxine withdrawal is safe. In this situation, the reasons to withdraw include cost of medication and monitoring, plus the fact that taking medication did not help. Yearly follow-up studies identify any progression of subclinical hypothyroidism.

41. My TSH is 3.6 μU/ml and I have thyroid antibodies but am in otherwise good health. Should I take thyroid hormone?

The answer is no. Here are the reasons. The only known consequence of having thyroid antibodies is the development of overt hypothyroidism. This occurs at a very slow rate at about 4.5% per year for individuals whose TSH is between 4.6 μU/ml and 10 μU/ml. If you have a TSH between 2.5 uU and 4.5 μU/ml and no thyroid antibodies, the rate is even slower, at 2.5% per year. If you were followed over 20 years, there is about a 50% chance that you might develop overt hypothyroidism. That means that 20 years from now, there is a 50% probability that your TSH will still be around a similar value of 3.6 μU/ml. Instead of starting thyroxine to prevent overt hypothyroidism (which requires blood drawings at least every 12 months to monitor replacement), I recommend thyroid function studies (free T4, TSH) every 1 to 3 years as an alternative. This approach avoids treating someone whose thyroid function may remain stable for decades without any consequences.

42. I have all the symptoms of hypothyroidism, yet my T4 and TSH are normal. I have read that I could have low T3 levels and might suffer from decreased conversion of T4 to T3 causing my symptoms. What about this possibility?

The symptoms of hypothyroidism are quite non-specific, probably because the thyroid affects almost all organ systems. No specific test or assay defines the action of thyroid on tissues. The closest evaluation of thyroid action is based on TSH secretion. The pituitary senses T4 levels, converts T4 to T3 intracellularly, and then increases or decreases TSH release (Question 4). Thus, we are left with measuring the levels of thyroid in the blood (more or less the messengers of thyroid action) and not the thyroid's direct effect on tissues. Why not measure serum T3 or free T3 since that is the most active hormone within cells? If low, then use T3 to replace thyroid hormone action. Serum T3 levels are uniformly elevated in untreated hyperthyroid patients. However, in half of the patients with overt hypothyroidism (low T4 levels and raised TSH levels), serum T3 levels are normal or mildly elevated (see Question 43). To put it another way, if one used low T3 levels alone as the biochemical marker of hypothyroidism, only about half of hypothyroid patients would be treated. Moreover, low T3 levels are a sentinel marker of euthyroid sick patients (see Question 14) who have no intrinsic thyroid disease. If serum T3 is not trustworthy in patients with documented hypothyroidism and low in patients who have thyroid function that returns to normal, why would you want to use it as a basis for treatment of patients with normal thyroid levels? These disparities compound and confound any reason to use T3-supplementation with symptoms of hypothyroidism without low T4 and elevated TSH levels.

Some patients have pituitary resistance to T4 (that is, failure to convert T4 to T3 at the level of the pituitary gland). This is a **familial** trait. These patients have elevated TSH levels because there is little intracellular T3 activity. The high levels of TSH cause hyperthyroidism in those with intact thyroid glands. If you are taking levothyroxine due to hypothyroidism secondary to Hashimoto's thyroiditis or I-131 treatment, you have had documentation of an elevated TSH associated with low T4 levels in the past. This means your pituitary sensed low T4 levels and did not convert enough T3 within the pituitary, causing an increase in TSH. There is no reason to presume that mechanism is not still intact. To answer your question, until there are means to assess thyroid hormone action directly on tissues, physicians will continue to debate using T3. Those who would use T3 do so with great conviction and some testimonials as to its success.

Familial

Hereditary; processes that cluster or run in families.

43. If T3 is so important in thyroid metabolism, why are T3 levels normal or elevated in half the patients with documented hypothyroidism?

T3 is very important in thyroid action. Most T3 comes from the peripheral conversion of T4 to T3; that is, one iodine molecule being clipped off to form T3. When T4 secretion falls as a result of autoimmune thyroid disease, TSH secretion increases exponentially. The increase in TSH induces a preferential increase in the secretion of T3 by the remaining thyroid cells. In addition, the conversion rate of T4 to T3 in other tissues (the brain in particular) increases, leading to a relative overproduction of T3 compared to T4 to restrict the impact of thyroid hormone deficiency on the body. This explains why serum T3 levels early in the course of hypothyroidism are normal or slightly elevated when the serum T4/free T4 levels are low and TSH is elevated. Over time, as T4 levels continue to fall, serum T3 levels also decrease to below normal. All this reflects an adaptive mechanism to blunt the effect of hypothyroidism on the body. So, using T3 levels to make a diagnosis of hypothyroidism depends on the time course of the disease process. Early in the course (subclinical hypothyroidism), serum T3 levels are often increased or normal. Then, as the mass of thyroid cells decreases, serum T3 also decreases. Again, TSH levels are elevated and increase progressively as serum T4 falls. Elevated serum TSH remains the best laboratory marker of hypothyroidism (except in central hypothyroidism—Question 15).

44. My baby tested positive for hypothyroidism at birth and was diagnosed with congenital hypothyroidism. What is congenital hypothyroidism?

If one ever wanted to see the dramatic effect of thyroid upon our bodies, the best place to look would be young infants born with no thyroid or those whose thyroid gland cannot produce enough thyroid. Thyroid hormone promotes nerve development and bone growth. In the absence of thyroid, children are usually normal in appearance at birth. That's because the mother's thyroid (T4) crosses the placenta in a limited amount. A baby born without a thyroid has about ⅓ the serum level of thyroid hormone compared to its mother. Fetal tissues convert maternal T4 to T3, which has more biological activity than T4, making for near normality at birth. However, the lack of thyroid becomes apparent after the first weeks postpartum, leading to the diagnosis of congenital hypothyroidism. These children do not grow (failure to thrive); their faces puff up; and the skin becomes dry. The neurologic consequences are devastating: dull, not crying, sleeping excessively, and failing to meet normal developmental goals. Basically, these children lose IQ and suffer with mental retardation. They wind up as cretins (dull, flat, mentally retarded dwarfs). Congenital hypothyroidism affects about one in four thousand births. The good news is that this condition is totally treatable. Thyroid replacement started in the first few days after birth prevents both mental and growth retardation. Successful therapy is one of the most rewarding conditions in medicine from the perspective of a physician who has seen untreated congenital (neonatal) hypothyroidism literally disappear.

Congenital hypothyroidism affects about one in four thousand births. The good news is that this condition is totally treatable. Thyroid replacement started in the first few days after birth prevents both mental and growth retardation.

That's because all infants born in civilized societies are screened for hypothyroidism Since screening for congenital or neonatal hypothyroidism began in the mid-1970s. Ideally, a TSH/T4 is checked 48–96 hours following delivery. A small sample of blood is placed on filter paper and sent to a central lab for testing. Each state sets its own protocol for testing TSH or T4. A low T4 and an elevated TSH (greater than 40 μU/ml) establishes the diagnosis for congenital hypothyroidism, which requires an immediate response in the form of thyroid supplementation. The earlier the diagnosis, the better our chance to prevent mental retardation. TSH levels following birth are much higher than adult levels and are in the adult range by 5–6 weeks postpartum. Values of TSH between 20-40 μU/ml are suggestive for hypothyroidism requiring repeat testing. About 10% of children with borderline elevated TSH levels develop hypothyroidism, necessitating lifelong thyroid replacement. If your baby screens positive for hypothyroidism, however, it may not mean hypothyroidism because the heel stick filter paper is just a screening study. Confirmation is necessary. Follow-up with a pediatric endocrinologist assures the best treatment regimen for your baby. Levothyroxine therapy is the standard prescription for congenital hypothyroidism.

45. I want to take thyroid to promote my metabolism. What can I do?

Inherent in this question are misconceptions about metabolism and the belief that thyroid supplementation fixes such problems. Many people assume that their low energy and fatigue, inability to lose weight, low body temperature, etc. relates to a metabolic problem that can be corrected by taking thyroid. If only that were the case! Such people are looking for answers and are basically looking under the wrong rock. If thyroid function studies (T4 and TSH) are normal, that means taking thyroid preparations to correct these symptoms is doomed to failure. The reason is that when one starts taking thyroid by mouth, the pituitary senses the increased thyroid levels and decreases TSH output, causing your own thyroid to decrease thyroid production. That's a protective mechanism to prevent a hyperthyroid state. If one ingests too much thyroid, then compensatory response is overwhelmed. Being mildly hyperthyroid has its virtues (more energy, eating without weight gain, etc.) but too much of a good thing can be devastating (fast heart rate, palpitations, tremulous, "wired", not able to sleep, etc.). Thyroid supplementation, when used appropriately in treating hypothyroid individuals, can be life-saving, but when used inappropriately, can become a treacherous medication.

Thyroid supplementation, when used appropriately in treating hypothyroid individuals, can be life-saving, but when used inappropriately, can become a treacherous medication.

46. Mrs. Lobaugh, since you had a thyroidectomy for treatment of thyroid cancer, how has your life been "living without your thyroid?"

Mrs. Lobaugh's comments:

I can honestly say that, after the initial treatment period, my life has been remarkably and thankfully unchanged by my diagnosis of thyroid cancer and subsequent thyroidectomy. Other than the requirement that I remember to take my thyroid pill each morning (which was a challenge until I purchased a compartmented 2-week, Monday–Friday pill box!), there have been virtually no effects on my life or lifestyle. I suppose I do have a slight scar in the crease of my neck; though it began as a red streak, it has healed to white and is barely noticeable. As with any scar, I apply extra sunscreen to that area in summer. I also schedule a yearly checkup with my endocrinologist to measure thyroglobulin levels (which should remain undetectable to indicate the absence of any thyroid tissue) and have a manual exam of my neck to check for lumps. As with the annual mammogram or periodic colonoscopy, you have to endure a little anxiety before hearing the 'all clear'.

47. What has been your experience taking thyroid supplementation?

I have met many people who struggle with thyroid problems—either too much thyroid hormone (hyperthyroidism) or too little (hypothyroidism). Perhaps a silver lining to having had a total thyroidectomy (removal of my entire thyroid) is the ease of maintaining a 'normal' level of thyroid hormone! I take a single, small (inexpensive!) pill each morning (in my case, 125 μg) and my serum thyroid hormone level remains stable at a normal value. Those thyroid cancer patients who retain some functioning thyroid tissue have a bit more of a challenge, as the supplemental thyroid hormone dose must be balanced with the variable levels of hormone produced by the remaining thyroid tissue. As long as your thyroid hormone level remains normal, your energy level remains normal, and you have no symptoms of a thyroid disorder.

In addition, thyroid hormone levels drop very slowly when you stop taking your thyroid pills. Consequently, there is no noticeable effect on my thyroid hormone level on those occasions when I inadvertently forget to take my morning pill, or forget to take my pills on an overnight trip out of town.

PART THREE

Hyperthyroidism

What is Graves' disease?

What are some of the facts about Graves' disease?

What are symptoms of an overactive thyroid (hyperthyroidism)?

More . . .

48. What is Graves' disease?

Graves' disease

An autoimmune condition in which increased levels of thyroid cause hyperthyroidism, which may also present with prominent and protruding eyes and changes over lower legs and feet called pretibial myxedema.

Although the name sounds foreboding, **Graves' disease** does not lead to the grave. The name, Graves, comes from the famous Irish physician, Robert James Graves who, in 1835, described "three cases of violent and long palpitations in females, in each of which the same peculiarity presented...enlargement of the thyroid gland." Dr. Caleb Parry had described a similar condition 10 years earlier, noting protrusion of the eyes as part of the syndrome. Because Parry was lesser known, the English literature has traditionally given credit to Dr. Graves, who was a well-known lecturer of medicine at that time. In 1840, Dr. Carl Basedow, a German physician, described the triad of goiter, palpitations of the heart, and exophthalmos (bulging eyes); so, in Europe the name Basedow's disease is synonymous with Graves' disease. Patients with Graves' disease present with an overactive thyroid (hyperthyroidism—see Question 50), diffuse enlargement of the thyroid (goiter—see Question 9), and prominent eyes (see Question 66), although the eyes may not be part of the presentation. Pretibial myxedema (non-pitting edema of lower extremities, usually found in patients who have eye disease) is a rare manifestation of Graves' disease (see Question 55). Another name for Graves' disease is diffuse toxic goiter.

49. What are some of the facts about Graves' disease?

Graves' disease is not a reportable disease and people rarely die with this disease. Most patients are never hospitalized. We do know it is a common condition, affecting about four people in a thousand. Females are 7–10 times more likely than males to develop Graves' disease. As with other thyroid diseases, its propensity for the feminine gender is not understood. The incidence peaks between the ages of 20 and 40; it's rare under age 10 and somewhat less common in the elderly. Family history of Graves' occurs in up to 50% of patients. There seems to be no racial preference for Graves' disease. Spontaneous remissions without treatment occur—the incidence varies 10–30% (cause for remissions remains unknown).

50. What are symptoms of an overactive thyroid (hyperthyroidism)?

The symptoms of hyperthyroidism are similar regardless of the cause. Because thyroid affects almost every organ system, **thyrotoxic** symptoms encompass a wide range of manifestations, each contributing to a clinical picture that is rarely mistaken when all the components are present. Most symptoms relate to the stimulatory nature of excessive thyroid hormone. Classic symptoms are listed in order of frequency: nervousness and anxiety (80–99%); increased sweating (50–91%); heat intolerance (41–89%); palpitations (63–89%); shortness of breath (66–81%); fatigue and weakness (44–88%); weight loss (52–85%); menstrual irregularity (45–80%); increased appetite (11–65%); eye symptoms (50%); and increased bowel frequency (12–33%). Many factors contribute to how each person presents with hyperthyroidism, including age, mode of onset, and individual sensitivity of each person's tissue to excessive thyroid levels. For example, the symptoms tend to be less severe when the onset of hyperthyroid is gradual. Younger individuals often tolerate hyperthyroidism without many complaints. Elderly patients often present with cardiovascular changes (atrial fibrillation and heart failure) and less with the adrenergic symptoms such as nervousness and anxiety. When someone tells you that they are eating well and not gaining weight, think of hyperthyroidism (uncontrolled diabetes mellitus is another possibility).

Thyrotoxic

Thyrotoxlc symptoms are hyperthyroid symptoms and can encompass a wide range of manifestations. Hyperthyroidism and thyrotoxicosis are often used interchangeably

51. What are signs of hyperthyroidism?

Typical thyrotoxic signs include thyroid enlargement (goiter—see Question 10), eye signs (stare, infrequent blinking, or bulging—see Question 66), inability to sit still and tremor (handwriting difficult to perform, shaky hands, etc.), moist and warm hands (such patients often radiate heat without having a fever), smooth and soft skin, and finally rapid heart rate (tachycardia and/or atrial fibrillation). In contrast to the symptoms which are not specific for any one cause of hyperthyroidism, signs may help identify the particular cause of thyrotoxicosis. About 95% of people with Graves' disease present with a diffuse goiter (both lobes and isthmus enlarged) that may be quite obvious or be palpated by your physician. Most patients with thyroiditis do not present with a goiter. Irritated eyes that protrude indicate Graves' disease. Mild thyrotoxic signs may be seen with thyroid adenoma that presents as a nodule or an enlargement of one thyroid lobe.

52. What are the causes for hyperthyroidism (thyrotoxicosis)?

Classical symptoms and signs of hyperthyroidism are unmistakable. Measuring T4 and TSH levels confirm the diagnosis. A careful history and physical examination with addition of a few lab studies identifies the cause of hyperthyroidism. **Table 5** lists the causes of hyperthyroidism. Most patients with Graves' have symptoms for several months; those with thyroiditis usually have symptoms for a few weeks. However, in both of these hyperthyroid states, the lab studies are identical (both have increased free T4 and low TSH). Hyperthyroid

Table 5 Causes of Hyperthyroidism

1. Graves' disease
2. Thyroiditis
   - a. Subacute/painless thyroiditis
   - b. Post-partum thyroiditis
   - c. Post-partum thyroiditis
   - d. Amiodarone-induced thyroiditis
3. Toxic multinodular goiter
4. Toxic adenoma (single hyperactive nodule)
5. Exogenous hyperthyroidism (thyroid medications, extra iodine)
6. Rare causes include TSH-secreting pituitary adenoma, trophoblastic tumors, struma ovarii (hyperthyroid tissue in ovary), and functioning thyroid carcinoma

individuals with diffuse toxic goiter often have proportionately higher T3 levels compared to T4 levels than those with thyroiditis. The definitive study is radioactive iodine uptake at 24 hours. The I-123/I-131 uptake is high in diffuse toxic goiter and low (or non-detectable) in thyroiditis. The uptake is also low in patients who are taking excessive thyroid hormone. **Figure 17** shows scans of a normal thyroid (panel A) and a hyperthyroid gland (panel B). Note the size and intensity of the hyperthyroid gland in comparison to the normal thyroid. The patient in panel B had a toxic diffuse goiter characteristic of Graves' disease. **Figure 18** shows scans from two hyperthyroid patients who had a toxic multinodular goiter (panel A) and a single toxic adenoma (panel B). Note that the overactive nodule leads to suppression of activity of thyroid in the remaining gland because those areas are not being stimulated by TSH. Remember, TSH levels are low in hyperthyroidism.

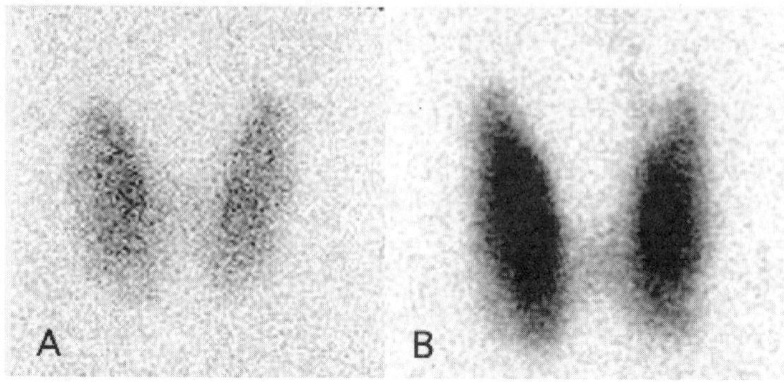

Figure 17 Thyroid scans showing a normal gland (A) and a diffusely hyperactive gland (B).

Note the darkest reflects increased activity and the increase in size of the hyperthyroid gland compared to the normal thyroid.

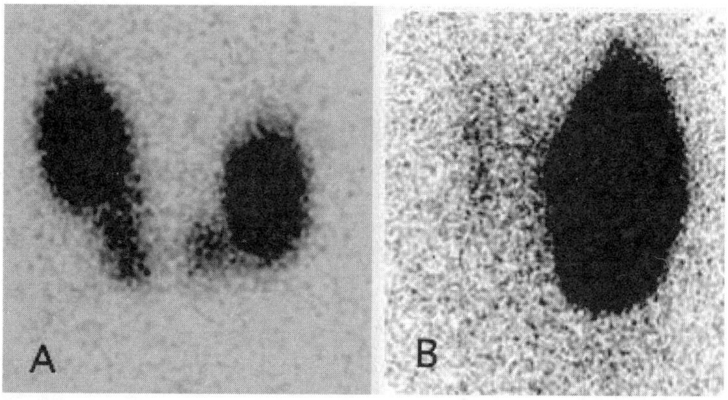

Figure 18 Thyroid scans demonstrating a toxic multinodular goiter (A) and a single toxic adenoma (B).

Panel A shows several hot areas. The "hot" area in the left lobe in panel B suppresses uptake of the remaining tissue in the right lobe so that side is not well visualized.

53. What is subacute thyroiditis?

Subacute thyroiditis involves a destructive process of the thyroid, causing release of stored thyroid hormone. As a result, patients present with thyrotoxic symptoms that include nervousness, tremors, rapid heart rate, palpitations, etc., all typical of classic hyperthyroidism. There are three types. The most common by far is silent, or painless, or subacute thyroiditis caused by an autoimmune process that is identical to Hashimoto's thyroiditis with lymphocytic infiltration of the thyroid. This is the same process as post-partum thyroiditis (see Question 71). It runs a similar course, presenting initially with hyperthyroid symptoms for about three months, then a recovery stage of **euthyroidism** (normal thyroid levels) which may be followed by transient hypothyroidism (but it can be permanent in about 5–10% of patients) until a euthyroid state is reached several months later. Painless thyroiditis rarely recurs in contrast to post-partum thyroiditis where it may recur following future pregnancies. Thyroid antibodies such as anti-TPO are usually positive. Another type of subacute thyroiditis is painful post-viral thyroiditis that follows a respiratory illness. Its hallmark is a tender neck and, on occasion, a swollen thyroid gland. It, too, is a self-limited illness. Anti-inflammatory meds help with the pain. Finally, a destructive form of thyroiditis can be found in patients who take amiodarone. In each of these instances, the radionuclide uptake (I-123, I-131, or $^{99m}TcO_4^-$) is low, in contrast to patients who have Graves' disease in which the uptake is quite elevated. Subacute thyroiditis rarely requires any specific intervention, although beta-blockers can be prescribed to alleviate symptoms of hyperthyroidism.

Euthyroidism

Normal thyroid levels.

54. What causes Graves' disease?

We know much about Graves' disease, but the underlying cause has not been established. Graves' disease is an autoimmune disease in which the thyroid is the main character. A specific part of our immune system is activated in which lymphocytes and mononuclear cells make an antibody that interacts with the TSH receptor on the thyroid cell. The TSH receptor normally binds TSH made by the pituitary. This TSH activation of the receptor causes the thyroid cell to make and release both T4 and T3. In Graves' disease, thyroid stimulating antibodies (in contrast to TSH) activate the TSH receptors, causing the thyroid to grow (leading to a goiter) and to produce excessive thyroxine (causing hyperthyroidism). The eye disease, also an immune phenomenon, is less well understood but probably does not involve the same TSH-receptor antibody. We do not know what triggers our immune system to start this process of Graves' disease. Some propose stress as a factor but that has not been proven. Women who are in their first year post partum are 4 to 8 times more susceptible to Graves', probably due to rebound of the immune system following pregnancy. Understanding that the thyroid responds to a "turned on" immune system by doing just what it is told is an important concept. Spontaneous remissions of the hyperthyroidism relates to the switching off of the immune system with disappearance of thyroid-stimulating antibodies.

We do not know what triggers our immune system to start this process of Graves' disease. Some propose stress as a factor but that has not been proven.

55. What are the complications of hyperthyroidism?

Because the thyroid affects almost all body tissues, one could expect multiple organs to demonstrate complications of excessive thyroid levels. **Table 6** lists many of these complications.

The heart rate normally increases, but up to 5% of hyperthyroid patients develop atrial fibrillation (irregular rapid heart beat) that decreases cardiac output causing more fatigue, shortness of breath, decreased exercise tolerance, etc. Blood flow stagnates because the atrium is not

Table 6 Complications of Hyperthyroidism

Circulatory System	Atrial Fibrillation
Musculo-skeletal System	Decrease Muscle Mass
	Osteoporosis
	Periodic Hypokalemic Paralysis
Nervous System	Delirium
	Thyroid Storm
Eye	Thyroid Eye Disease
Skin	Pretibial Myxedema

emptying its blood efficiently into the ventricles, predisposing one to clots which can move out of the heart into other organs. These mobilized clots (emboli) often go to the brain causing strokes, the most serious complication of atrial fibrillation. The incidence of atrial fibrillation increases with age, as does the risk for stroke. If an elderly person develops atrial fibrillation, your physician may consider anticoagulation treatment. Following treatment of the hyperthyroid state, most patients (60–70%) revert back to a normal sinus rhythm within 3 months after developing normal thyroid levels (euthyroid state). Hyperthyroid patients who remain in atrial fibrillation may be candidates for electrical **cardioversion**.

Following treatment of the hyperthyroid state, most patients (60–70%) revert back to a normal sinus rhythm within 3 months after developing normal thyroid levels (euthyroid state).

Cardioversion

Electrical shock across the chest wall to reset the heart rate to normal sinus rhythm.

Hyperthyroidism affects bone metabolism. Increased bone resorption and bone turnover cause more calcium to leach out of bony tissue. On rare occasions, serum calcium levels are elevated, but urine calcium levels are universally increased (sometimes kidney stones are formed). Prolonged duration of untreated hyperthyroidism leads to **osteoporosis** (loss of bone mineral content) and possible increased fracture rate. After successful treatment of hyperthyroidism, bone heals and bone mineral density increases but not always to normal.

Osteoporosis

Loss of bone mineral and bone integrity that may lead to fracture.

Muscle mass and strength decrease in a hyperthyroid patient. Some hyperthyroid patients lose so much muscle that getting up from a chair or commode is a struggle. Rarely, Asian men develop muscle paralysis associated with low serum potassium as a consequence of hyperthyroidism. Once a euthyroid state is reached, these muscle problems resolve.

Questions 66 and 67 discuss thyroid eye disease and Question 65 talks about thyroid storm.

Finally, the skin may display a rare complication of Graves' disease called pretibial myxedema. Large patches of orange-peel-appearing skin on the lower legs are unsightly but cause little harm. This manifestation of Graves' disease occurs primarily in those patients with Graves' eye disease. Larger accumulations of this tissue lead to tuberous pretibial myxedema (see **Figure 19**). Unfortunately, there is little effective treatment for this condition.

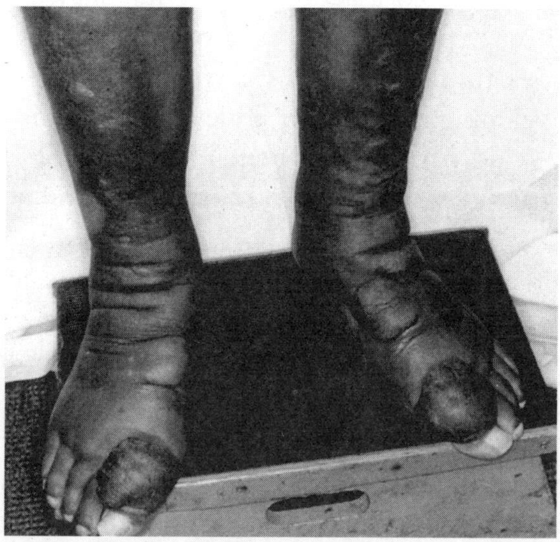

Figure 19 Patient with pretibial myxedema (nodular form).
Deposits of mucinous tissue under the skin leads to these changes. This patient had long-standing Graves' eye disease as well.

56. *My physician diagnosed me with hyperthyroidism and has ordered a thyroid uptake and scan. What do these studies mean?*

The thyroid avidly traps iodine, both the stable and naturally occurring I-127 and the radioactive **isotopes** (I-123 and I-131). Because these isotopes emit irradiation, nuclear scanning of the thyroid can measure uptake and detect areas of decreased or increased uptake on a scan. The procedure for a thyroid uptake requires administering a tracer dose of I-123 (200 μCi) or I-131 (50 μCi) by mouth and then measuring radioactivity 24 hours later by putting the counter over the anterior neck. Normal uptake is 10–30% of the original activity administered. Hyperthyroid patients with Graves' disease or toxic nodular goiter have elevated values. Hyperthyroid patients with subacute thyroiditis or iodine-induced hyperthyroidism have low uptake. Knowing these results establishes a specific cause for the hyperthyroidism. In addition, the thyroid also traps **pertechnetate** (similar to iodine). $^{99m}TcO_4^-$ (radioactive pertechnetate) allows for excellent imaging (scan) and limits the amount of radiation exposure (1 rad to thyroid). A scan captures the distribution of radio-labeled isotope on a photographic image (see **Figure 17**). $^{99m}TcO_4^-$ must be given intravenously and the scan performed about 30 minutes later. For scanning, I-123 is often used. The radiation exposure for a scanning dose of I-123 (2.6 rad to thyroid) is much less than I-131 (65 rad to thyroid). The type of radiation produced by I-131 gives scans of poor quality.

Isotope

One or more atoms having same atomic number (protons) but different molecular weights (neurons).

Pertechnetate

A coumpound containing the TcO_4^- compound.

57. What is the treatment for diffuse toxic goiter (Graves' disease)?

Actually, there are several treatment options. Most thyrotoxic patients with symptomatic palpitations, racing of the heart (tachycardia), nervousness and anxiousness, tremors, and sweating respond well to taking a beta-blocker (propranolol, metoprolol, atenolol, etc.). These adrenergic symptoms of "flight or fight" decrease rapidly, but not altogether, once these medications are begun. Symptoms return as soon as the beta-blocker is stopped as long as the hyperthyroid state exists. It's important to remember that, in Graves' disease, the thyroid is doing just what it's told by the immune system. Some people with Graves' will experience spontaneous remission of their disease; most will not, and will therefore need some intervention. Think of the thyroid as a car with the horn stuck on. The horn is constantly bellowing (loud and annoying, not allowing anyone to be at ease). The ideal way of dealing with the horn is to take your hand off of the steering wheel or kill the electrical supply to the horn. For the Graves' patient, that means telling the immune system to stop making antibodies that are stimulating to the thyroid. Unfortunately, at the present time that is not possible. Someday, there may be means to turn specific immune functions off and on, but not today. That means to fix the loud, boisterous horn, we could pour water on the horn, shoot the horn, or take the horn out. The best way to remember the therapeutic options that affect thyroid function is what I call the 3 B's: a bottle of pills, the buzz of radioactive I-131, or the blade of the surgeon.

Pouring water on the horn to cool it off is analogous to the bottle of pills. These are anti-thyroid medications such as propylthiouracil, methimazole, or in Europe, carbimazole, a drug that is converted to methimazole. Over time, these drugs decrease thyroid hormone production and, as a result, the thyrotoxic symptoms abate. I liken these meds to putting a lid on a pot of boiling water: the steam goes away, but once the lid is removed, the steam bursts forth as long as the burner is on. These meds control the hyperthyroidism; they do not cure it, similar to taking high blood pressure medications. Stopping your anti-hypertensive leads to the return of hypertension. See Question 58 for pros and cons of this therapy.

Shooting the horn is similar to buzzing the thyroid with radioactive iodine because most thyroid glands literally die from the irradiation. I prefer the term "buzz" rather than "nuke" to ablate the thyroid. Radioactive iodine is quite effective and is likely to produce a permanent "cure." It takes care of the hyperthyroidism but only in trade for a lesser problem—long-term hypothyroidism. See Question 61 for pros and cons of this therapy.

Surgery (affectionately known as the blade) to remove the overactive gland is historically the oldest form of specific treatment of hyperthyroidism, dating from the late 1800s. At that time, surgical mortality was high because of the lack of preoperative preparation to reach a normal thyroid state. Subtotal thyroidectomy is still used in specific circumstances such as pregnancy. See Question 69 for pros and cons of this therapy. **Table 7** reiterates the treatments for Graves' disease.

Table 7 Treatment for Graves' Disease

The 3 B's—Bottle, Buzz, or Blade
1. Bottle of Pills (anti-thyroid medications)
2. Buzz of Radiation (I-131 therapy)
3. Blade of Surgeon (thyroidectomy)

58. What are the pros and cons for using anti-thyroid medications to treat hyperthyroidism?

Since the 1940s, anti-thyroid medications (bottles of pills) have effectively controlled the thyrotoxic state. Hyperthyroid patients usually reach a euthyroid state within 6–8 weeks of starting these drugs. Your doctor will start with a higher dose and then reduce the amount to a maintenance dose once the serum thyroxine is normal. Methimazole and propylthiouracil (PTU) work quite well. Most physicians (and patients) prefer methimazole because of its once-a-day dosing with 1–3 tablets (10–30 mg) each day. Methimazole (on a mg basis) is more potent than PTU. PTU comes in only one dose (a 50-mg tablet). Because of its short half-life, PTU must be administered three times a day. The initial dose (300–900 mg a day) means you take 2 to 6 tablets in divided doses three times a day (6 to 18 tablets a day). In addition, PTU tablets are as bitter as gall. Physicians often prefer PTU to treat thyroid storm (see Question 65) and to manage hyperthroidism during pregnancy. Infants whose mothers took methimazole (and carbimazole) during their entire pregnancy may suffer very rare birth defects (scalp, throat, or anal complications). However, many countries, including Japan, have only methimazole available. Patients who are allergic to methimazole may also be tried on PTU.

Methimazole is taken for 12–18 months. Blood studies are necessary at least every three months to monitor thyroid levels and to prevent over-treatment with methimazole causing hypothyroidism. During this time, most patients feel normal. While taking the medication, some people develop a skin rash or itching which is usually transient and responds well to antihistamines. If these symptoms continue, switching to PTU may help. Methimazole could be taken longer were it not for the rare allergic reaction of **agranulocytosis** in which low white blood counts lead to infection, sore throat, mouth ulcer, fever, and possible death. The agranulocytosis, occurring in about 1 in 500 patients, comes "out of the blue" without any warning. Stopping the methimazole reverses this process. Should you develop any of these symptoms, stop taking the medication and see your doctor, who will get your white blood count measured. If the count is normal, you may resume the methimazole. Again, long-term use of **antithyroid medication** (in contrast to anti-hypertensives or statins) is to be avoided.

Agranulocytosis

A rare allergic reaction (due to long-term use of Methimazole) in which white blood counts lead to inflection, sore throat, mouth ulcer, fever, and possible death.

The only way to know whether the hyperthyroidism has remitted while taking methimazole is to discontinue the medication (methimazole withdrawal). Statistically, about 10–30% of hyperthyroidism remits while on antithyroid medication. Symptoms of thyrotoxicosis recur in 70–90% of patients a few weeks after the methimazole is stopped. That's because the autoimmune process causing the hyperthyroidism still persists.

Antithyroid medication

Drugs that block thyroid hormone production, such as methimazole or propylthiouracil (PTU).

59. Are there any indications that predict that Graves' disease might not remit spontaneously, even after treatment with antithyroid medications?

No one can predict the course of untreated Graves' disease. As noted previously, only 10–30% of Graves' disease goes away on its own. Clinical experience leads one to make a few general observations about the natural history of Graves' disease, but none of the following are set in stone. Patients with a strong family history of Graves' (mother, sister, grandmother, or aunt) are not likely to remit permanently with medications. Patients with large goiters who have had hyperthyroid symptoms for many months (though untreated) are not likely to have remission, even though antithyroid medication will control the hyperthyroidism. Patients who have high concentrations of TSH receptor-stimulating antibodies are less likely to remit than those with lower levels of these antibodies. Finally, Afro-Americans who often have a more aggressive disease (larger goiters and higher level of receptor antibodies) rarely have spontaneous remission of their hyperthyroidism.

60. Are there any forms of hyperthyroidism for which antithyroid medications are not particularly helpful?

Any hyperthyroid state in which the thyroid is making and releasing thyroid hormones (both T4 and T3) responds to propylthiouracil (PTU) or methimazole. These drugs block the synthesis of T4 and T3. Hyperthyroid states, such as thyroiditis, hyperthyroidism due to taking too much thyroid supplements, or amiodarone-induced hyperthyroidism (particularly type II) do not respond to these drugs.

61. What are the pros and cons for using radioactive iodine to treat hyperthyroidism?

Since the 1940s, radioactive I-131 has been used to treat Graves' disease (and toxic nodular goiter as well). Some physicians do not use it for patients younger than 18 years of age, but many do. Concerns about birth defects, increased miscarriage rates, or bodily harm-causing cancer have not materialized. Many publications document the safety of such treatments for thousands of patients. The amount of radiation to the ovaries for someone receiving a typical dose of I-131 to treat thyrotoxicosis is equivalent to having an abdominal CT scan or barium enema. In some studies, Graves' eye disease seems to be exacerbated following radioactive I-131. Women who are pregnant or nursing should not receive any radioactive iodine because the baby's or infant's thyroid traps I-131, leading to possible hypothyroidism.

Radioactive iodine is not the "magic bullet," but it is close. It is simple, safe, and effective and is given in the outpatient setting. Because only the thyroid traps iodine to any extent, radioactive iodine is used to spare other tissues from injury. I-131 emits short-ranged beta particles that destroy or severely injure thyroid follicular cells (1–2 mm from source) causing them to die over a period of several weeks. A typical treatment dose for hyperthyroidism is 5–15 mCi. It is given orally in a single dose as a capsule or liquid. I-131 is absorbed by the stomach and duodenum and circulates to the thyroid. What is not trapped there is excreted in the urine. The treating physician determines the amount of I-131 administered by considering the size of the thyroid and its 24-hour uptake. Administering a lower dose of I-131 hoping to avoid hypothyroidism usually translates into persistent hyperthyroidism and the need for repeated I-131 treatment. Most physicians give just enough to make you hypothyroid. For a few days following this treatment, the anterior neck may be sore (in my experience, this occurs in less than 5% of such treated patients). It takes 4–8 weeks to achieve a euthyroid state (normal T4 levels). By 10–14 weeks following treatment, more than 80% of patients are hypothyroid (low T4 and raised TSH). Once TSH is above 10 μU/ml, one starts lifelong thyroid supplementation, which is the major complication of this therapy. About 5% of I-131-treated patients remain persistently hyperthyroid and need a second dose about six months following the initial dose. In conclusion, I-131 treatment is safe, effective and definitive, and relatively cheap (about 10 times less than surgery).

Radioactive iodine is not the "magic bullet," but it is close. It is simple, safe, and effective and is given in the outpatient setting.

62. I am scheduled to take I-131 treatment for hyperthyroidism and I had a friend who had been treated with I-131 for thyroid cancer. What are the risks from the radiation of such treatments?

These are legitimate concerns for anyone receiving I-131. Over the last 70 years, more than two million people in the United States, have been treated with radioactive iodine (I-131) for both hyperthyroidism and thyroid cancer. Thus, there is a wealth of information about possible side effects from radiation exposure. I-131 treatments are safe and effective. Concerns about genetic mutations have been muted. The number of miscarriages, birth defects, thyroid cancers, or any other cancers is not increased above the expected incidence for any of these disorders. Of course, all sources of radiation are potentially hazardous (even sunlight), so undue exposure is to be avoided. Understanding the amount of radiation received helps immensely. The average citizen receives about 3 mSv each year from atmosphere, earth, etc. Any additional exposure comes from medical procedures (chest X-ray, CT scans, etc.). For example, a chest X-ray is about 0.02 mSv; skull X-ray, 0.07 mSv; IV urogram 2.5 mSv; upper GI exam, 3.0 mSv; CT head, 2.0 mSv; barium enema, 7.0 mSv; and abdominal CT 10 mSv. The average amount of radiation received to the body after I-131 for hyperthyroidism varies slightly depending on dose, but averages around 30–35 mSv. The gonads receive a total dose of 10–15 mSv, about the equivalent of an abdominal CT exam. So the amount of total body irradiation received from I-131 therapy is not excessive and is in the same range as many radiographic procedures whose safety is generally taken for granted.

63. If I take I-131 to treat my overactive thyroid, will I gain weight?

Hyperthyroidism increases the rate of metabolism, causing the body to burn up food more rapidly than normal. In many hyperthyroid patients, appetite and food consumption are also increased. Because of individual differences in metabolism and appetite, most hyperthyroid patients lose weight, some maintain their weight, and some actually gain weight. Those who eat well yet lose weight "get away with murder." I call this: "dishonest weight loss." When they are cured by any method of treatment, body metabolism decreases and food is burned more slowly. Appetite usually decreases as well, and most patients return to their pre-hyperthyroid weight. However, the increased appetite may persist longer than the increased metabolism. To avoid weight gain, one must decrease the food intake or increase caloric expenditure (exercise) or a combination of ingesting fewer calories and exercise. Radioiodine treatment cures the hyperthyroidism, lowers thyroid hormone levels, and thus causes symptoms to disappear. Weight gain is not an inevitable consequence of treatment.

64. I recently was diagnosed with hyperthyroidism and treated with I-131. My hair is coming out by the handfuls. Is this hair loss related to the I-131 treatment?

The answer is yes...and no! Hair grows in cycles. Each hair progresses through a growth stage, a resting stage, and a dying stage. At all times, some of your hair is young and growing, some long and mature, and some dying and falling out. Most of our hair is in the resting stage of the cycle. Any process that causes these hairs to get into the same phase of growth (in synch) means that at the end of the cycle more hair than normal falls out. Post-partum hair loss following weeks after delivery exemplifies a normal physiological model of excessive hair loss. Pregnancy causes much of the hair to get into the same growth stage and at the end of the cycle, there is abundant hair loss. Thyroid disease (both hyperthyroidism and hypothyroidism) and illnesses in general affect hair growth by putting much of your hair in same growth cycle. At the end of the cycle, there is resultant hair loss. The reason for hair loss in your situation was not a direct effect of radioactive I-131 on the hair follicle, but rather an indirect effect on correcting the hyperthyroidism which had put many hairs in the same growth cycle. So that is the reason for the yes-and-no answer.

65. What is "thyroid storm?"

"Thyroid storm" is a rare complication of hyperthyroidism in which the symptoms of hyperthyroidism are greatly exaggerated. Cardinal signs necessary for this diagnosis include fever, altered mental status (confusion, delirium, or even coma), severe tachycardia (often with atrial fibrillation), and gastrointestinal symptoms (diarrhea, vomiting, and possibly jaundice). Often some stress, such as pneumonia or surgery, precipitates the thyroid storm in an individual who was not previously diagnosed with hyperthyroidism. The diagnosis of thyroid storm is a clinical one made by the physician because the results of blood studies are similar to those of hyperthyroid patients without these severe symptoms. Thyroid storm is rarely seen today because most hyperthyroid patients are already diagnosed and treated.

Historically, mortality was up to 50%, which is partially responsible for the name, "thyroid storm." Such patients need hospitalization and intensive medical therapy.

66. What is thyroid eye disease?

When anyone presents with prominent or bulging eyes, this raises the question of thyroid eye disease. The medical term that indicates thyroid eye disease is Graves' eye disease or Graves' ophthalmopathy. The prominent eyes may result from staring, which gives the appearance of bulging eyes, or from actual forward movement of the eyeball (**proptosis** or **exophthalmos**), or combination of the two. Thyroid eye disease usually affects both eyes, but occasionally only one eye is involved. Staring, as seen when one is frightened, results from increased muscle tone of the upper eyelid muscles which are innervated by sympathetic nerves. Any increase in thyroid hormone levels causes the sympathetic nervous system to be turned up a notch or two, leading to a faster heart rate, more perspiration, and fine shakes or tremors. In essence, an accentuation of the "flight or fight" response of the sympathetic nerve system causes the stare or glazed-eyes. The stare, though not noticeable to the individual, may be brought out by looking up and then downward. The eyelid will often hang up or lag behind the eyeball, showing the characteristic lid lag that physicians notice during a physical exam. The stare usually goes away when the thyroid levels return to normal. However, most patients with thyroid eye disease actually have forward protrusion of the eyeball, given the characteristic finding as shown in **Figure 20**. Women are about six times more likely to have thyroid eye disease than men, mainly because hyperthyroidism due to Graves' disease is more prevalent in women. That

proptosis or **exophthalmos**

The forward movement of the eyeball or bulging eyes.

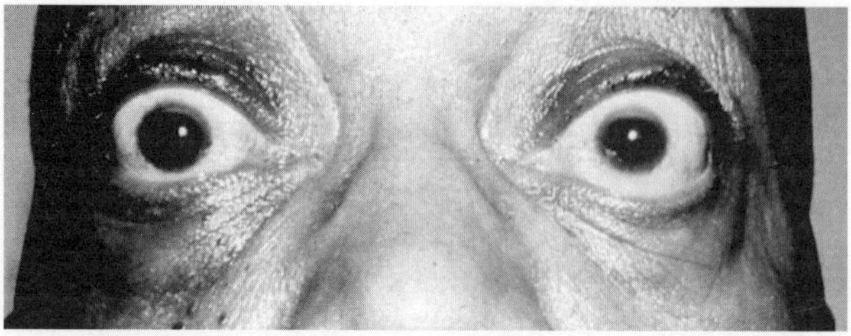

Figure 20 Graves' eye disease with proptosis.
Large protrusion of the eyes are classic for Graves' disease. Often, these patient's eyelids do not close completely while sleeping leading to exposure and dryness of the cornea.

being said, men often have a more severe form of this disorder. For whatever reason, smoking increases the risk of thyroid eye disease some eight-fold. The incidence of thyroid eye disease depends largely on what criteria one uses to make the diagnosis. A stare is common in hyperthyroidism, but proptosis is much less common (maybe 5–10% of Graves' patients). If all hyperthyroid patients with Graves' disease had CT scans of the orbits, then up to 40% may have findings such as minor muscle hypertrophy even though there may be no clinical signs or symptoms. If only one eye is affected, one must rule out other causes of proptosis, including orbital or retro-orbital tumors.

67. What causes thyroid eye disease?

We know much about thyroid eye disease; however, the specific cause or causes are not known. An autoimmune disorder that is not related to a specific infection or trauma appears to be the underlying cause. A low-grade inflammatory response to the tissues surrounding the eyeball includes the **conjunctiva** (transparent skin over the front of the eye), the muscles that move the eye,

Conjunctiva
Transparent skin over the front of the eye.

and any contents that occupy the bony orbit in which the eyeball resides. The actual eye and its contents, such as the iris, lens, retina, and vitreous humor (jelly-like material between the lens and retina) are not directly affected by this process. Remember, the space where the eye sits is surrounded by bone; the eyeball is literally a sphere sitting in a bony cone. Any increase in the size of the soft tissues and eye muscles leads to the eye moving forward because that is the only free space. The inflammatory response causes the conjunctiva to be injected and become edematous, leading to the red or "pink eye" and baggy eyelids (see **Figure 21**). The eyes may not blink as much, and that causes dry and irritated eyes, often with more tearing. Eyelids that do not close completely while blinking or at night when sleeping may result in significant drying. This in turn causes more irritation. The inability to close the eyes completely is called **lagophthalmos** ("rabbit eyes") and may lead to corneal abrasion and possible loss of sight. The ocular muscles swell and often do not work as well, leading to inability to focus or to double vision (**diplopia**). If these muscles compress or infringe on the optic nerve, then visual loss—the most serious complication of this disease—is possible. Fortunately, this is quite uncommon.

Lagophthalmos

The inability to close the eyelids completely.

Diplopia

Commonly known as double vision; the simultaneous perception of two images of a single object.

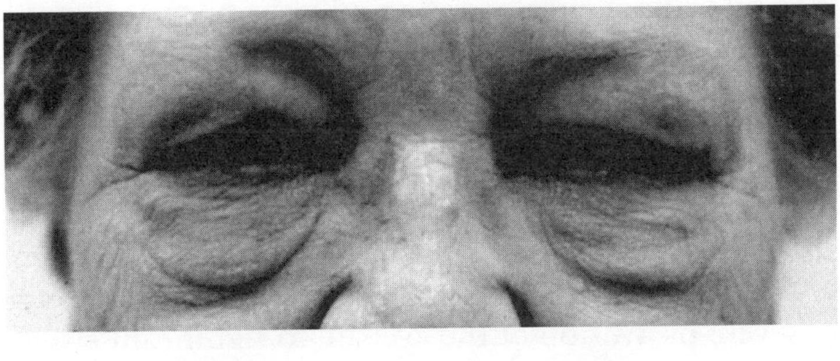

Figure 21 Graves' eye disease with periorbital edema.

This black and white photo does not reflect the redness associated with the inflammatory and edematous condition that this patient had. The eyelid puffiness seen in hypothyroidism does not show this inflammatory response.

68. I have been diagnosed with thyroid eye disease (Graves' eye disease). What can I expect from this disease and how is it treated?

This inflammatory process, leading to thyroid eye disease, is a fickle process. Most patients (> 90%) who present with prominent eyes, with or without double vision, have hyperthyroid symptoms that come on about the same time as the hyperthyroidism. In others who present only with hyperthyroidism, the eye disease comes months to years later, after the overactive thyroid has been successfully treated and when the thyroid levels are normal. A few people come in with only Graves' eye disease, before any symptoms of hyperthyroidism, and with normal thyroid levels. Then, months to a couple of years later, they develop an overtly overactive thyroid gland. So, thyroid eye disease is related to the thyroid, but it is not a cause-and-effect relationship. I tell my patients, "the eye disease and the thyroid disease run in the same stream like fish, but do not have to run in schools or be directly related. Both share the same water." The other 10% of people with thyroid eye disease may have hypothyroidism due to Hashimoto's thyroiditis or be clinically euthyroid with normal thyroid levels for many years.

Our expectations about the success of any specific therapy rest on understanding the nature and course of thyroid eye disease.

Our expectations about the success of any specific therapy rest on understanding the nature and course of thyroid eye disease. As previously noted, the spectrum of thyroid eye disease varies considerably from just a stare, to mild to severe protrusion of the eyeball, to significant swelling of muscles causing diplopia, to corneal abrasion that could lead to infection and non-healing due to continued exposure, and even to blindness due to compression of the optic nerve. Finding a knowledgeable physician who can manage the likely concurrent hyperthyroidism is an important first step. Establishing normal thyroid levels improves the stare, once the hyperthyroidism is controlled. Also, the euthyroid state ensures that whatever course the eye disease takes, it's not related directly to poorly controlled thyroid levels. If there is protrusion (proptosis), then one needs an experienced ophthalmologist who deals with this disorder. Often, nothing is needed other than good follow-up with the ophthalmologist. Down the road, surgery may be necessary, and having someone who knows your particular situation is invaluable. Minimizing exposure of the eyes to the sun, wind, snow reflection, and bright lights helps immensely with the symptoms of irritation. Good sunglasses that wrap around the face and cover the lateral portions of the eye are a necessity. Using liquid tears often aids the dryness symptoms. Your physician may recommend raising the head of your bed (2″ bricks placed under bed posts work well here) to lessen the edema that may accumulate while sleeping. Diuretics may be tried, but usually do not help. A beta-blocker such as propranolol or atenolol may decrease the stare, but does nothing for protrusion. Maintaining a euthyroid state over time is the best medicine for thyroid eye disease. When managing the eyes, the course is measured in months and years, not days or weeks. This is one time that the patient needs to be patient. For patients with protrusion and evidence of corneal abrasion, eyelid surgery (**blepharoplasty**) to reduce the eyelid opening helps. For patients with double vision (diplopia), using prism glasses (lenses that bend light rays) helps, particularly if the divergence of the eyes when looking forward is minor. Of course, blocking vision in one eye by using an eye patch or a lens covering over glasses fixes the diplopia. Once the diplopia is stable for many months, then surgery to lengthen or shorten the particular eye

When managing the eyes, the course is measured in months and years, not days or weeks. This is one time that the patient needs to be patient.

Blepharoplasty

A functional or cosmetic surgical procedure intended to reshape the upper or lower eyelid by the removal and/or repositioning of excess tissue as well as by reinforcement of surrounding muscles and tendons muscles can be performed by an ophthalmologist experienced in this form of surgery. Often, this surgery is combined with blepharoplasty. Rarely, some patients with thyroid eye disease develop loss of vision in one or both eyes due to optic nerve damage (mostly secondary to pressure on the nerve going to the retina). This is an emergent situation requiring the services of the treating physician and ophthalmologist. You need to see these doctors immediately to preserve vision! Usually, the physician administers high dose steroids in the hope of lessening inflammation and edema pressing upon the optic nerve. If the vision worsens significantly in a few days, then the ophthalmologist will operate to remove bone about the orbit which allows more space for the orbital contents and reduces pressure on the optic nerve. Again, loss of vision is a rare complication of thyroid eye disease requiring immediate attention.

69. How about surgery to treat hyperthyroidism?

For many years, subtotal thyroidectomy was the main treatment for Graves' disease. However, prior to introduction of beta-blockers and anti-thyroid medications, surgery was risky. Patients were prepared for a couple of weeks of iodine, which transiently and slightly decreased thyroid levels while also decreasing vascularity to the thyroid. Complications included bleeding, infection (no antibiotics available), and thyroid storm (see Question 65). Now, patients are made euthyroid prior to surgery and the risks are much, much less. Surgery is a good choice for those younger patients who have a single, toxic nodule causing the hyperthyroidism. Pregnant women who are hyperthyroid may have surgery during the second tri-semester, which has historically been the best time for surgery. Patients with toxic multinodular goiter, particularly if it is large and symptomatic, are candidates for surgery. Older patients with smaller goiters do well with I-131. Other conditions, such as amiodarone-induced hyperthyroidism (type 1) that fails to respond to anti-thyroid medications, are also surgical candidates (I-131 will not work for these people because the overactive gland does not trap the "hot" iodine). Complications of surgery relate directly to the experience of the surgeon. These include bleeding, hypocalcemia (hypoparathyroidism), injury to the recurrent laryngeal nerve causing hoarseness and possible loss of voice, and surgical hypothyroidism if too much thyroid is removed. Question 89 addresses these issues. Finally, surgery and anesthesia costs are considerable ($25,000). In contrast, I-131 treatment for hyperthyroidism is about $2,000.

Complications of surgery relate directly to the experience of the surgeon.

70. Considering the choices for treating my Graves', what do I have to say to my physician?

You need to read Questions 58, 61, and 69, so that you will have some background information about your treatment. Most physicians, including surgeons, are less likely to recommend surgery. If you see a surgeon first, you need to remember the axiom, "If you go to Midas, you are going to get a muffler." That is their training and background and what they know and do best. Surgery may be recommended for the patient who is allergic to anti-thyroid medications, those who have significant Graves' eye disease (who have been treated medically for a prolonged time until their eyes are stable), pregnant women who fail anti-thyroid medication (rare), and those with large bulky goiters (particularly if there are symptoms of airway obstruction). Most Graves' patients are managed medically at least for a while. In the United States, most endocrinologists recommend I-131 as definitive therapy unless you are pregnant. Much of this is based on the individual physician's experience, considering age, family history, race, and degree of hyperthyroidism. If you are unsure about taking I-131, pursue treatment with methimazole/PTU for a while before committing to the I-131 thyroid ablation. There is a 10–30% chance that your Graves' may remit while on this medication. That means a 70–90% chance you will not remit. Treating with an experienced physician who treats thyroid problems helps immensely. If you have significant Graves' eye disease, most doctors will treat you for 1–2 years with anti-thyroid medication instead of I-131 because there is a slight propensity for the eye disease to worsen following I-131 treatment. Even this is a difficult call, because thyroid eye disease has a "mind of its own" (see Question 68). After taking methimazole for a year or so, if the Graves' symptoms return following discontinuation of the medication, then I-131 is the best choice. **Table 8** lists the advantages and disadvantages of these treatments. **Figure 22** shows the effect of I-131 treatment upon goiter size. The goiter is no longer present.

71. I have been diagnosed with postpartum autoimmune dysfunction. What is postpartum thyroiditis?

Postpartum autoimmune dysfunction, the most common thyroid condition associated with pregnancy, affects 5–9% of women in the United States. It may also occur after miscarriage and should be considered in anyone with disturbed thyroid function within a year of delivery. During pregnancy, the immune system is quite tolerant

Table 8 Advantages and Disadvantages of Treatment Modalities for Graves' Disease

Treatment	Advantages	Disadvantages
Bottle of Pills (Methimazole or PTU)	No radiation	Frequent relapses
	No surgical risks	Requires frequent testing
	No permanent hypothyroidism	Occasional side effects/adverse reaction
Buzz of Radiation (Radioactive I-131)	Definitive treatment of symptoms	Delayed control of hyperthyroidism
	Easy to perform and fast	Decreased effectiveness with large goiters
	Outpatient study	Transient worsening of eyes
	Low cost	Permanent hypothyroidism
Blade of Surgeon (Thyroidectomy)	Definitive treatment of hyperthyroidism	Hypoparathyroidism (0.9–2%)
	Vocal cord/nerve injury (0.1–2%)	
	No radiation	Bleeding/infection/ anesthesia
	Immediate correction of hyperthyroidism	Scarring
		High cost
	Removal of large goiters	Inpatient surgery (overnight stay)

and does not normally reject tissue (embryo/baby) that has half of someone else's chromosomes. Basically, the rejection system is "on hold." Once the baby is delivered, the mother's immune system is hyper-responsive and often the thyroid is the target of its inflammatory

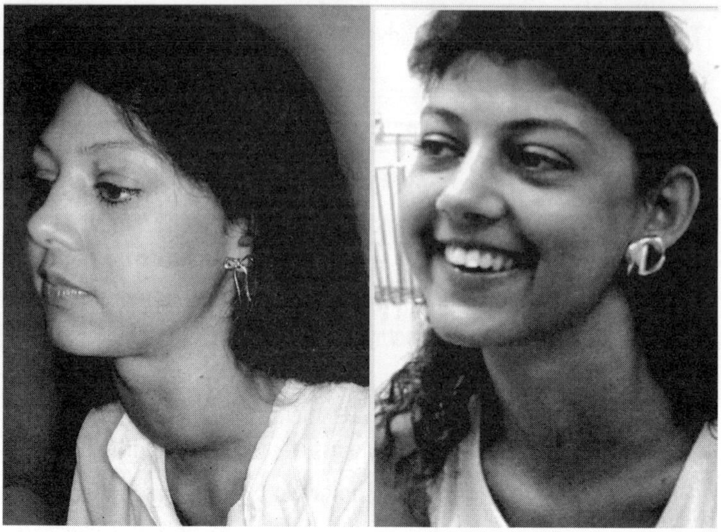

Figure 22 Effect of I-131 on goiter in treatment of hyperthyroidism. This patient presented with a diffuse toxic goiter (left panel). She received I-131 therapy. The right panel shows the same patient about six months later with total resolution of her goiter.

response. Postpartum thyroiditis has the same cellular response as Hashimoto's thyroiditis (see Question 25). Abundant levels of anti-TPO antibodies are a hallmark feature. There is destruction of thyroid follicles releasing stored T4, causing hyperthyroidism. The process is usually painless and rarely associated with a goiter. The hyperthyroid symptoms might be attributed to taking care of a newborn with little sleep, anxiousness of a new arrival, etc. The diagnosis of postpartum thyroiditis could easily remain unrecognized or actually be missed. That's because the hyperthyroid phase of postpartum thyroiditis lasts 2–3 months, with return to normal thyroid or slightly low thyroid status, all of which is usually resolved by six months. If enough thyroid cells are destroyed, hypothyroidism develops. This may be transient or permanent. **Figure 23** outlines these stages of post-partum thyroiditis. Most physicians would treat

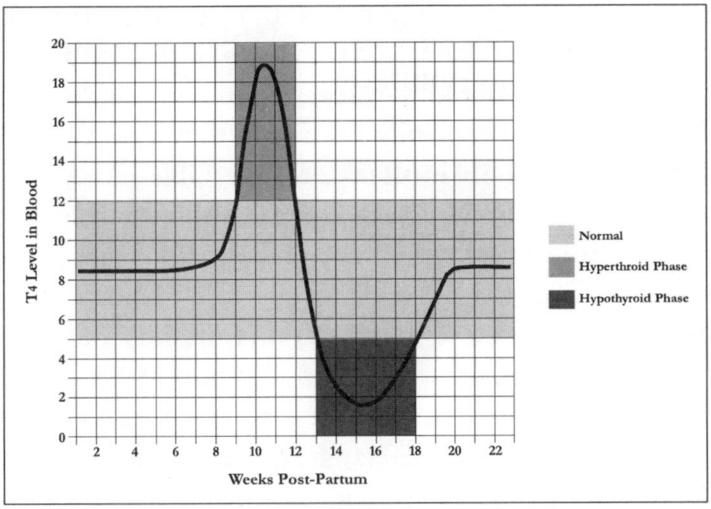

Figure 23 Course of post-partum thyroiditis.
Serum T4 levels rise usually peaking 8–12 weeks post-partum, followed by a few weeks of normalcy, then transient low levels for a few weeks with recovery. Not all patients recover to normal and will need thyroid supplementation.

with levothyroxine for a year or two, then withdraw to see if this hypothyroid stage is permanent. This avoids replacing thyroxine for life. If the hyperthyroidism lasts more than four months, then the likely diagnosis is Graves' disease, which would require specific therapy. The good news for most postpartum thyroiditis patients is that it is transient and requires no specific therapy. However, watch out for the next pregnancy; post-partum thyroiditis often repeats itself.

72. What is subclinical hyperthyroidism?

Subclinical hyperthyroidism is essentially a laboratory diagnosis based on finding a suppressed TSH in the presence of normal levels of T4 and T3. The increased sensitivity (ability to measure smaller and smaller amounts of TSH) of current assays has identified many more people with TSH below the normal reference range. These individuals have no to little symptoms that can be attributed to excessive amounts of thyroid. These lab results generally surprise both the patient and physician. The TSH is often non-detectable and usually less than 0.1 μU/ml (normal range 0.4–4.5). Subclinical hyperthyroidism affects 1–2% of the adult population and up to 3% of those over the age of 80 years. Lower degrees of suppressed TSH (0.1–0.4 μU/ml) are more common. Again, serum T4 and T3 concentrations are in the normal range in all of these people. If the T4 and T3 were above the normal range, the diagnosis would be overt hyperthyroidism, which is associated with a plethora of symptoms and signs (see Questions 50 and 51).

73. My physician found my TSH to be low on routine studies. I do not feel unhealthy, so why now do I have the diagnosis of subclinical hyperthyroidism?

Subclinical hyperthyroidism, a diagnosis based on laboratory findings of a suppressed TSH in the presence of normal levels of T4 and T3, causes few if any clinical symptoms. Let's use this analogy. You are driving a car down the highway where the maximum speed limit is 55 mph. You are not paying close attention to the speedometer which may not be calibrated as well as it used to be. You may be going 54 to 58 mph; you can't tell for sure. You pass a patrolman who was clocking your speed with a radar gun. The display reads 56.6 mph. You are technically speeding. But again, riding in a car, it is difficult to discern whether you might be traveling at 54 mph or 55 mph or 56 mph or 57 mph or 58 mph; they are about the same to you. The TSH is the radar gun; it accurately assesses your thyroid function. If it says you are speeding above the speed limit, then you are, even though you perceive that you are perfectly fine and not running too fast. That is pretty much the same as with subclinical hyperthyroidism. The low TSH means your pituitary thinks you are speeding, but you sense that you are okay, mainly because your free T4/free T3 are normal. Remember the relationship of T4 to TSH (see Question 6); a small change in serum T4 creates a very large change in TSH values. For example, let's assume your serum free T4 is 1.0 ng/dl (normal reference range, 0.5–1.5 ng/dl) and your serum TSH is 1.0 μU/ml (normal reference range 0.5–4.6 μU/ml). If the free T4 goes from 1.0 ng/dl to 1.4 ng/dl (still within normal), your serum TSH falls from 1.0 μU/ml to 0.2 μU/ml—that's quite a drop and by the way, your TSH is now in the range to make the diagnosis of subclinical hyperthyroidism.

74. What are the causes of subclinical hyperthyroidism?

Again, even a slight increase in serum T4 or T3 causes the very sensitive pituitary thyrotroph to reduce TSH production, leading to lower TSH levels. The causes of increased T4/T3 levels are the same as those in patients who have overt hyperthyroidism. **Endogenous** (the thyroid itself releasing more thyroid) conditions include subacute thyroiditis (see Question 53), early onset of Graves' disease (see Question 48), toxic nodular goiter (see Question 52), and drug-induced hyperthyroidism (e.g., iodine, amiodarone, recent radio contrast material, etc.). The primary exogenous cause of subclinical hyperthyroidism is overtreatment with thyroid supplementation in patients previously diagnosed with hypothyroidism. TSH suppression is often the goal in treating thyroid cancer patients.

Endogenous
The thyroid itself releasing more thyroid.

75. What are the risks of subclinical hyperthyroidism?

Long term studies show the risk of subclinical hyperthyroidism developing into overt hyperthyroidism is low, at 1–3% per year. Patients with subclinical hyperthyroidism are at a slight risk for cardiac and bone loss. The risk of atrial fibrillation increases three-fold for those over sixty (only if TSH < 0.1 μU/ml), but not at all for those with levels of TSH 0.1–0.4 μU/ml. Some studies demonstrate improved heart ventricular function once the TSH is normalized. Bone loss is not a problem in premenopausal women, but post-menopausal women with subclinical hyperthyroidism appear to lose more bone. Bone mineral density increases once these women are treated; however, the risk for increase in their fracture rate in those women has not been established.

76. Who should be treated for subclinical hyperthyroidism?

Most people need periodic checkups every 3–6 months. Measurement of TSH, free T4, and free T3 identifies those who are progressing to overt hyperthyroidism. Prior to any treatment, the potential causes require investigation. Patients who are taking thyroid supplements ought to reduce the dose to normalized TSH (reasonable TSH goal; 0.5 to 2.6 μU/ml). Thyroid scanning with radioactive isotopes helps identify some causes (thyroiditis, Graves', toxic nodule, etc.). Often the uptake is in the upper limits of the normal range or quite low, with thyroiditis or exogenous thyroid administration). Again, a suppressed TSH is often a management goal for those with thyroid cancer. Patients with subclinical hyperthyroidism who develop new-onset atrial fibrillation, angina, or heart failure; accelerated loss of bone density; pre-menopausal females who develop menstrual irregularity or infertility; or non-specific symptoms of tiredness, frequent bowel movements, and palpitations associated with borderline high free T3 are candidates for treatment. There are no long term perspective studies to compare treatment modalities. For some, a trial of 6–12 months of anti-thyroid medications would be appropriate and for others, radioactive I-131 ablation would be favored. Still others with large, symptomatic goiters, might be treated with thyroid surgery. You should discuss these options with your physician, weighing the pros and cons for each treatment.

PART FOUR

Thyroid Nodule

What is a thyroid nodule?

Why should I be concerned about a thyroid nodule?

What is the best way to evaluate a thyroid nodule?

More . . .

77. *What is a thyroid nodule?*

Thyroid nodule

A lump, bump, or mass in the thyroid that may be large enough to feel (palpated) or too small to be felt and only seen with ultrasound; the nodule may be benign or malignant.

A **thyroid nodule** presents as a mass or lump in the thyroid. Such lumps may be discovered by the individual, family or friends, or palpated by the health care professional. A careful examination of the neck may identify up to 4% of the adult population with a thyroid nodule. Usually the thyroid nodule needs to be 1 cm (0.4 inch) in size to be felt or palpated. Many nodules are noted incidentally on ultrasound of carotids or CT/MRI of neck looking for other abnormalities. Thyroid nodules are so common that at least 50% of our population above the age of fifty have thyroid nodules noted with ultrasound or at autopsy. The nodule may be solid, cystic, or partially solid/cystic. Such nodules can be single or numerous ("multinodular"). Such multinodular thyroid glands often lead to enlargement of the thyroid which is called a multinodular goiter. Most patients with thyroid nodule(s) have thyroid function studies (TSH, T4) that are totally normal.

78. *Why should I be concerned about a thyroid nodule?*

Carcinoma

Another word for cancer.

Most of these nodules are harmless and benign, requiring no treatment. Small nodules (less than 1 cm) found on ultrasound are not worrisome. However, thyroid cancer presents as a thyroid nodule just as breast **carcinoma** may present as a lump or mass. Though the chance of cancer is low (less than 4%), the reality of thyroid cancer necessitates a good evaluation. You should see your physician if you have not already done so. Certain risk factors are troublesome for cancer. Radiation to the neck (treatment of tonsils and adenoids, etc., as a child) increases the risk of thyroid cancer that develops many years later, following exposure. Routine X-rays and dental studies have not proved to be problematic. If the nodule is hard or very firm (like bone); if your physician feels lymph nodes in addition to the thyroid nodule (possible spread to these areas); if your voice is hoarse (possible cancer invading nerve to larynx); or if you are a child, the cancer risk is higher.

79. What is the best way to evaluate a thyroid nodule?

The real concern is whether the nodule or nodules are cancerous. Nothing short of having tissue to specifically identify the cause answers the question as to what is taking place. Ultrasound of the thyroid reveals the shape, size, and number of nodules. Certain ultrasound characteristics are suggestive of malignancy (irregular borders, small **calcifications**, increased blood flow), but none are diagnostic. In the past, nuclear medicine scans were ordered because cancerous thyroid nodules did not trap or take up the radionuclide, leading to a "cold" or hypofunctioning nodule. **Figure 24** shows a "cold" nodule in the right lobe of the thyroid. The problem with this study is that > 80% of all thyroid nodules are "cold," and of these "cold" nodules, only 10% or so are malignant. The only time nuclear medicine scan helps is when the nodule takes up an increased amount of I-123. These "hot" or hyperfunctioning nodules are universally benign. Radionuclear scans are generally ordered when the TSH is suppressed. As noted previously, most patients with thyroid nodules have normal thyroid function studies, including TSH.

Calcifications
Tiny mineral deposits in thyroid tissue that may or may not represent cancerous tissue.

Your health care provider should refer you to a physician who has expertise in fine-needle aspiration (FNA) biopsies. FNA gathers tissue from the nodule. A small caliber needle (smaller in size than the usual venipuncture

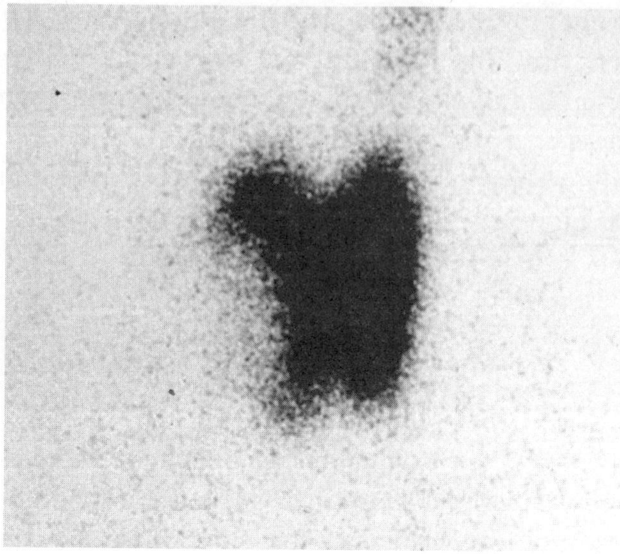

Figure 24 Thyroid scan showing hypofunctioning ("cold") nodule in left lobe.

There is an area missing on the lateral portion of this lobe corresponding to the "cold" nodule. At least 80% of thyroid nodules are "cold." Fine needle aspiration of such nodules identifies the cause.

needle) is inserted into the nodule and material is aspirated, placed on a microscope slide, and sent to cytology where smear is stained, and read by a **cytopathologist**. Most hospitals and reference labs have experienced cytopathologists who are critical to interpreting these findings. For non-palpable nodules, ultrasound-guided FNA ensures that the appropriate site is biopsied. This may take place in your physician's office or the radiology department of your clinic or hospital. You should ask the individual who is performing the FNA any questions you might have about the procedure. Several techniques are used for FNA. The procedure is generally brief, without too much discomfort, and is done while you are awake (either lying or sitting). The number of passes required to gather tissue depends on adequacy of the sample.

Cytopathologist

A doctor specifically trained to look at small amounts of tissue to determine what type of tissue is being examined.

80. What results can I expect from the fine-needle aspiration (FNA) biopsy?

Generally FNA results fall into four categories: benign, malignant, indeterminate, or non-diagnostic. On the average, 80% of FNA readings are benign (most often colloid nodules, **hyperplastic** nodules, etc.). About 5% are malignant (well-differentiated thyroid carcinoma, the most common by far; lymphoma; metastatic carcinoma to the thyroid; etc.). **Figure 25** shows the characteristic "Orphan Annie Eyes" seen in **papillary thyroid carcinoma**. These cells make an "easy" call for the cytopathologist for diagnosis of papillary thyroid carcinoma. About 5–10% of the specimens received are difficult to read and a specific diagnosis cannot be made from the cytologic features. For example, a very cellular specimen that has mostly lymphocytes may be from a lymphoma or from a process such as Hashimoto's thyroiditis, in

The only way to tell a benign follicular process from a malignant follicular process is to see whether the cells extend beyond the capsule of the nodule. This requires having the surgical specimen in hand.

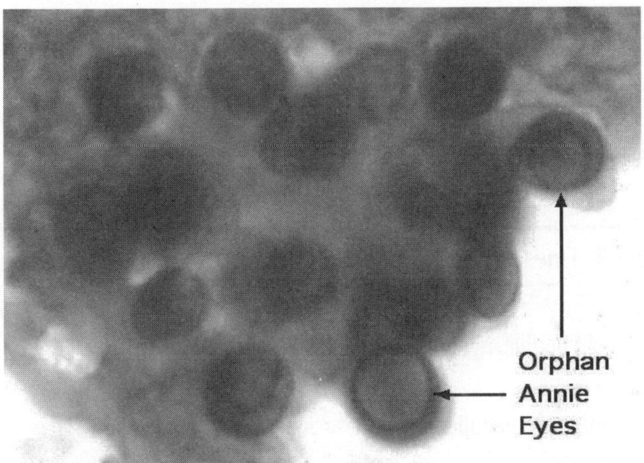

Figure 25 Fine needle aspiration cytology showing the "Orphan Annie Eyes" of papillary thyroid cancer.

The arrows show the bull's eye changes which are in stark contrast to normal thyroid cells, making this an easy diagnosis for the cytopathologist.

hyperplastic

An increased number of thyroid cells, often crowded in clumps.

Papillary thyroid carcinoma

The most common cause of thyroid cancer, distinguished by its microscopic features.

which lymphocytes abound. In specimens that contain abundant thyroid follicular cells, the cytopathologist cannot differentiate a benign follicular neoplasm from a thyroid follicular carcinoma because the cells are identical. The only way to tell a benign follicular process from a malignant follicular process is to see whether the cells extend beyond the capsule of the nodule. This requires having the surgical specimen in hand. Finally, non-diagnostic readings are caused by failure to obtain enough cells at FNA to make a call. Cysts are the culprits here because there may be a paucity of cells within the fluid. **Table 9** lists the possible results from a FNA.

Biopsy

A procedure in which cells are collected for microscopic examination

In the past, before there were good cytopathologists, some physicians and surgeons would **biopsy** with a large cutting needle to obtain a core of thyroid tissue. The amount obtained allowed sectioning of the specimen, which was read by a pathologist. This procedure has been all but abandoned because FNA yields good results, does not require as much technical expertise, and most importantly is associated with significantly fewer side effects (bleeding and pain).

Table 9 Fine Needle Aspiration Results

Benign (colloid nodule, hyperplastic nodule, lymphocytic, etc.)	80–85%
Malignant (papillary or medullary thyroid carcinoma, lymphoma, anaplastic)	5%
Indeterminant (follicular adenoma/follicular thyroid carcinoma, hypercellular nodules)	5%
Non-diagnostic (cysts, too few cells, etc.)	5–10%

81. Now that I know my FNA results, what should I do?

Obviously, the specific FNA results dictate the next step. You definitely need input from your physician. If the FNA results are benign, as they most often are, your physician usually suggests follow-up visits to assess the nodule. On occasion, thyroxine may be suggested (see Question 84). If cancer is found, referral to an experienced thyroid surgeon is mandatory. Make sure the surgeon specializes in thyroid cancer surgery; you will not regret traveling a little farther to get the best in your area. You will find that these surgeons work with endocrinologists and nuclear medicine physicians. This coordinated team approach provides you with the optimum of care. For indeterminate readings, particularly those in which the cytopathologist records "follicular neoplasm or follicular neoplasm cannot be excluded," I recommend thyroid surgery (again by an experienced thyroid surgeon) to remove the affected lobe for a definitive diagnosis. For those non-diagnostic results because of inadequate cellular material, repeat FNA often clears the confusion. If necessary, FNA with ultrasound guidance yields enough cells to make a diagnosis.

82. Mrs. Lobaugh, how did you find out about your thyroid cancer?

Mrs. Lobaugh's comments:

As is often the case, the discovery of my thyroid cancer was inadvertent. While brushing my teeth one morning, I noticed a small, pea-sized lump under the skin on my neck that rode up and down as I swallowed. The lump was not tender, but felt hard to the touch. The lump remained unchanged for several weeks, and I had enough scientific background to think that perhaps it was a thyroid nodule—though the thought of thyroid cancer did not cross my mind. I had no symptoms to indicate a thyroid imbalance of any kind.

I made an appointment with a friend who is an endocrinologist, and my level of concern rose somewhat as he suggested a "fine needle aspirant" (FNA) of the lump. This involved inserting a very fine needle through the skin of my neck into the lump, and removing some cells for microscopic examination. The procedure was done in my friend's office, and was a simple and minimally painful experience. The initial pathology report suggested that the cells were a bit abnormal, but not malignant. My endocrinologist, however, remained suspicious because of the solid feel of the solitary lump. A second FNA indicated that the small lump was papillary thyroid carcinoma.

83. I have had a FNA with benign results. Do I need another biopsy in the future?

If the clinical picture remains the same; that is, no growth or change in character of the nodule, then a repeat FNA seems unnecessary. Good follow-up visits every 6–12 months, along with thyroid ultrasound, allow you to follow this plan. However, any change dictates a repeat FNA. Cytopathologists are good at their jobs but there is about a 1.5–2% chance they missed the diagnosis by calling the nodule benign when, in fact, it was cancerous. If the aspirated area did not represent the lesion or the cancer was just a small part of a larger nodule, the specimen could be erroneously read as benign.

84. I have a benign colloid nodule and my mother had the similar problem. She took thyroid for years. Should I take a thyroid preparation?

In the 1950s, physicians started patients who had what they presumed was a benign nodule or multiple nodules on thyroid medication. The idea was that if one could put the thyroid at rest by supplying thyroid hormone via a pill, then the thyroid would not have to work or grow. The reasoning was similar to this: if you broke your ankle and put it in a cast and did not walk on it, the calf muscles would atrophy from disuse. So if the thyroid did not have to work, nodules might shrink, similar to muscle tissue. Thyroid hormone supplementation decreases TSH production, and thus leads to less thyroid stimulation. This therapy is called thyroid suppression treatment. Thyroid suppression was the only medical therapy available and was often used to see if the nodule would shrink. If the nodule enlarged while taking thyroid hormone, surgery to remove the nodule was performed. Remember, this was before FNA biopsy. On rare occasions, a nodule actually would decrease in size while using thyroid (levothyroxine) suppression, but most (99%) remained the same size. Thus, many patients remained on thyroid for years. There is no consensus about thyroid suppression these days. Generally it is not used. Committing someone to thyroid supplementation for the rest of their lives when the treatment may not help is one reason. The other is that as you get older (often above 50 years), these nodules may function autonomously; that is, they continue to function even with low TSH levels. The combination of these nodules producing thyroxine and the patient ingesting T4 orally often causes hyperthyroidism. My practice regarding thyroid suppression is not to start it in patients over fifty who have thyroid nodules or multinodular glands. For younger patients, I may try thyroid suppression for one year. Then, if the nodule decreases in size, stay on this regimen. If the nodule remains the same, I discontinue the levothyroxine. I do not want to commit someone to lifelong thyroid suppression when there is no evidence for its doing any good and too much thyroid may harm them.

85. I have a 2 cm left thyroid nodule that was read as "follicular neoplasm" on FNA. My surgeon says he is going to remove the left lobe. Why not just remove the nodule and spare the whole left lobe of my thyroid?

On the surface, removing just the nodule seems to be the right thing to do. However, there are at least two good reasons to remove the entire left lobe of your thyroid. The thyroid gland is quite vascular. Trying to dissect out the nodule is likely to create a bloody mess. The cut gland will ooze profusely and stopping it by cauterization is not practical. To make the procedure relatively bloodless, the surgeon identifies, isolates, and ties off the arteries and veins that supply each lobe of the thyroid (in this case only the left inferior and superior thyroid arteries and veins). Then the thyroid can be mobilized and the isthmus cut and ligated to remove the entire left lobe. As noted in Question 80, the only means to differentiate a benign follicular neoplasm from a malignant follicular neoplasm is to examine the capsule and see whether these cells (which are identical to each other on FNA) invade and go outside the capsule of the nodule. Just removing the nodule would not allow the pathologist to make this distinction. Also, if the nodule proved malignant, cancer cells would have been dispersed by cutting into its margins. If the nodule was indeed malignant, the entire lobe needed to be removed anyway. Finally, to answer the question about preserving function by leaving or not removing thyroid tissue, you do not have to worry. The remaining lobe, if healthy, serves one quite well. We only need about 20% of our thyroid gland to work in order to maintain normal thyroid status. Similar to other organs, we are endowed with plenty of reserve. For example, you can donate a kidney (if the remaining one is healthy) and still maintain normal kidney function.

86. How did you feel and how did you handle being diagnosed with thyroid cancer?

Mrs. Lobaugh's comments:

My initial response to the diagnosis of thyroid cancer was disbelief, tempered by a healthy dose of fear. My father had passed away the previous month after a valiant and heart-breaking 10-month battle with esophageal cancer, and the diagnosis of "cancer" was terrifying. I suppose I went through all the expected emotional stages: disbelief, anger, sadness and acceptance, but each of these feelings was enveloped in a blanket of fear generated by the word, "cancer".

As a research scientist by training, I needed information. I wanted to know what I should expect in terms of treatment and long term prognosis, though I was afraid of what I might learn. My endocrinologist assured me that thyroid cancer was both treatable and, in many cases, curable. Armed with this reassurance, I gathered information from reliable sources (I strongly recommend accessing internet information only from credible sources), and learned what I could about this disease.

At the same time, I gathered personal resources. The support of my husband, family, friends and faith community was invaluable as I faced this unexpected challenge.

87. What did you tell your family and children about your cancer?

Mrs. Lobaugh's comments:

At the time of my diagnosis, my two sons were 9 years and 23 months old, and my daughter was 5 years old. They had just lost their grandfather to esophageal cancer, so the "C" word was never used with the kids. Mommy had to have some 'surgery' and 'treatment' for a lump on her throat – end of story. We would not have lied in response to a direct question, but fortunately, many children are involved in their own world, and do not pry into the adult arena. I still marvel that earlier this year when the subject came up, my now 13-year-old daughter looked at me and said, with deep concern on her beautiful face, "I didn't know you had thyroid cancer!" I believe all parents need to evaluate the age and maturity of their children in determining when, and how much, to tell them about a cancer diagnosis.

My adult family members had just been through the ordeal of my father's struggle with esophageal cancer and eventual death, so it was also very difficult to tell them about my diagnosis. Fortunately, I could begin with the good news that in all likelihood, the surgery and subsequent treatment would cure me of the disease. I told my close friends the truth, as well, as I didn't want to leave them to wonder if I had encountered pirates to acquire the slash across my throat that was all too evident immediately after the surgery!

88. What are the indications for thyroid surgery?

Most thyroid operations relate to the removal of a large, symptomatic goiter, the treatment of hyperthyroidism, or the follow-up management of a thyroid nodule. Though a goiter may be unsightly, large goiters rarely cause symptoms. That's because goiters can enlarge without impediment, moving forward and laterally. However, if the thyroid enlargement proceeds down into the inlet of the chest, then there is little space to grow or move. This space is fixed by the bony margins of the sternum, cervical ribs, and vertebra and is already occupied by the trachea, esophagus, and the great vessels coming out of the chest. The downward extension of these goiters acts as a "cork in a wine bottle's neck" and presses against these vital structures. These goiters are often called substernal goiters. Patients with large multinodular goiters that are causing symptoms like shortness of breath or difficulty swallowing are candidates for thyroidectomy. Such patients are likely to be elderly and have substernal extension of their goiters, leading to compression and/or narrowing of the trachea.

Hyperthyroid patients with an autonomous functioning adenoma (toxic thyroid adenoma) often undergo surgery for this condition. Hyperthyroid patients with large goiters are also surgical candidates. Sometimes, physicians refer the pregnant hyperthyroid patient to the surgeon if there is intolerance/allergy to medication. Hyperthyroid patients should be nearly euthyroid prior to surgery to prevent surgical complications including "thyroid storm."

Patients with suspicious or malignant FNA biopsies are routinely referred for thyroidectomy. The only cure for thyroid carcinoma is removal of the cancerous gland. Surgeons differ about the amount of thyroid to be removed, but generally a thyroid thyroidectomy (both thyroid lobes and isthmus) is performed for malignant thyroid nodules greater than 1.5 cm ($^5/_8$ inch) in diameter. For well-differentiated thyroid carcinomas less than 1 cm, a lobectomy without removal of the opposite lobe is all that is necessary. Such small tumors are called microcarcinomas.

The surgeon who does one or two thyroid operations a year has many more post-operative problems than a surgeon who does one or two of these surgeries a week. The word here: experience counts!

Patients with unsightly nodules or large goiters may have thyroid surgery for esthetic reasons, realizing that most insurance companies consider this plastic surgery and do not cover its cost.

89. What are the possible complications of thyroidectomy?

Thyroid surgery is a relatively uncommon operation. Many patients with thyroid nodules, who in the past would have had surgery, now have **fine needle aspiration** to make a diagnosis. This has led to fewer thyroidectomies and fewer surgeons who perform this operation. Complications following thyroid surgery are generally rare when the procedure is performed by an experienced surgeon. The surgeon who does one or two thyroid operations a year has many more post-operative problems than a surgeon who does one or two of these surgeries a week. The word here: experience counts! Make sure your surgeon has plenty of thyroid experience. If not, seek another surgeon.

Fine needle aspiration biopsy

Using a thin needle to collect fluid or cells directly from a mass or nodule for microscopic evaluation.

Several complications are possible: bleeding/infection, vocal cord paralysis/injury, low serum calcium (hypocalcemia), anesthesia death, keloid formation, and permanent hypothyroidism. Bleeding, if it occurs, is within a few hours following surgery. Many surgeons wait up to 6 hours before discharging patients, and some prefer to have their patients stay overnight just to make sure that no large **hematoma** (blood clot) develops in the operative site to compromise breathing. Infection, though quite rare, develops within a few days post-op. Vocal cord paralysis from injury to a laryngeal nerve causes hoarseness or, more commonly, loss of high pitch tones. Because there are two nerves, each supplying one vocal cord on each side, total vocal paralysis is extremely rare because both nerves would have to suffer damage. Many surgeons use the latest technology of recurrent laryngeal nerve monitoring during thyroid and parathyroid surgery. A special endotracheal tube that has electrodes to sense current going to each vocal cord muscle. If the nerve is manipulated, a change is noted, helping the surgeon avoid injury to the nerve. The endotracheal tube from anesthesia may cause swelling of the vocal cords, leading to transient hoarseness without any injury to the laryngeal nerves. Hypocalcemia (for symptoms, see Question 19) is also rare because all four of the parathyroid glands (two on each side) would need to be damaged (surgical hypoparathyroidism). These parathyroid glands are small and fragile, having a blood supply similar to a cherry attached by its long stem. Injury by just manipulating the artery (stem) may cause parathyroid damage, even though the parathyroid gland(s) was left intact. If surgery involves removing only one lobe, post-operative hypocalcemia does not occur. Hypocalcemia is much more likely following a total thyroidectomy (1 to 7 percent of such patients develop this complication—the experienced surgeon having less). The

Hematoma
Blood clot.

management of surgical hypoparathyroidism may be difficult, requiring calcium and vitamin D. Death related to anesthesia (1 in 200,000 operations) often is not considered by the patient as a risk factor for surgery, and is more likely in the seriously ill patient. Some patients are more prone to form keloids at the site of skin closure. Hypothyroidism is an expected complication following near total or total thyroidectomy. This requires lifelong thyroid supplementation.

90. What are some of the facts about thyroid cancer?

Anaplastic

Aggressive cancer cells that lose the distinguishing characteristic of the original tissue.

Thyroid cancer is an uncommon form of cancer, representing 1–2% of all cancers. More than 32,000 cases of thyroid cancer are diagnosed yearly in the United States. Thyroid cancer has several pathological types: papillary, follicular, medullary, and **anaplastic**. The thyroid may harbor lymphoma and metastatic cancer as well. The types of thyroid cancer vary in frequency and aggressiveness. The papillary and follicular types are well-differentiated and by far the most common (90 percent of the cases), with the least aggressiveness and best long-term prognosis. The medullary type forms about five to ten percent of thyroid cancer, with intermediate aggressiveness and prognosis (see Question 100). Fortunately, anaplastic thyroid carcinoma is the rarest (1 percent), but it is quite aggressive, leaving the lifespan measured in a few months. Because the well-differentiated thyroid cancers have such a good prognosis with treatment, 330,000 patients in the United States are followed for their cancer. Thyroid cancer occurs in both men and women, and at any age. Women have three times the risk as men. For whatever the reason (probably better detection), the number of new cancer cases diagnosed each year is increasing. The aggressiveness of thyroid cancer increases with the age of the individual. Papillary thyroid cancer in a 65- to 70-year-old person acts quite differently than the same tissue type in a 20- to 30-year-old individual.

91. I am a 25-year-old mother of two who was just diagnosed with papillary thyroid carcinoma. My entire thyroid was removed with a 2.5 cm cancer in the right lobe and a small 2 mm focus in the left lobe with one of three lymph nodes containing cancer as well. What is my prognosis?

Well-differentiated thyroid carcinomas have an excellent prognosis. A patient under 45 years old with a papillary thyroid carcinoma that has not grown through the thyroid capsule can expect a 99% chance of a 25-year survival rate, even when local lymph node metastases are present. This assumes good medical follow-up and treatment with thyroxine. Still, the recurrence rate approaches 10–30%, with the most common site being the lymph nodes on the side of the original tumor. The fact that bilateral disease and a positive lymph node were present does not affect long-term prognosis. There is a greater chance of local recurrence in the previously described case. The prognosis worsens significantly if there is extension of tumor into surrounding tissues, tumor size greater than 4 cm, distal **metastasis** to lung, bone, or brain, or if the patient is over 45 years of age.

Metastasis, metastasize

Spread of cancer.

92. Mrs. Lobaugh, how was your thyroid cancer treated?

Mrs. Lobaugh's comments:

Approximately 2 weeks after my diagnosis of papillary thyroid carcinoma, I underwent neck surgery to remove my thyroid gland (total thyroidectomy, in my case) and examine nearby lymph nodes for evidence of metastases (fortunately, none was found). This was followed 3 months later with a high oral dose of radioactive iodine (100 mCi I-131) to destroy any remaining thyroid cells (thus minimizing the chance that these cells could be, or become, malignant). Finally, 20 months later I had a whole-body scan following administration of a small oral dose of radioactive iodine.

The thyroidectomy was not difficult as surgeries go. I was resigned to losing my thyroid gland, but was deeply concerned that the surgery would damage my laryngeal nerves and end my career as an amateur choral singer. I hedged my bets by the choice of an experienced and talented surgeon, and the surgery was completed without damage to my vocal chords or delicate parathyroid glands.

I woke up after surgery to feel a pressure on my neck—as if someone was pressing a hand on the juncture of my neck and chest. The pressure was caused by the dressing, and was more uncomfortable than painful. I spent one night in the hospital, then returned home to the care of my wonderful husband. I spent a day or two taking it easy—then slowly resumed my normal activities (as slowly as is possible with three young children). When the dressing was removed, I had a red slash in the natural crease across my neck, and I made numerous tasteless jokes over the next few days about having my throat slit... Over the course of the next few months, the scar faded and several years later is barely noticeable.

For a month prior to receiving the treatment dose of radioactive iodine-131, I stopped taking my thyroid pill to decrease my circulating thyroxine level in order to stimulate uptake of the radioactive iodine by any residual thyroid cells. I was warned by my endocrinologist that, as my thyroid hormone levels dropped, I might experience symptoms of hypothyroidism; including fatigue, muscle stiffness and joint pain, cold intolerance, constipation and forgetfulness. Although my thyroxine decreased to undetectable levels, I experienced very mild symptoms of hypothyroidism, and was able to maintain my normal schedule with just a bit more fatigue than normal.

By far the strangest part of the treatment was the treatment dose of radioactive iodine. As a scientist, I had often used radioactive iodine in the course of my research. I would receive 1 mCi of radioactive iodine encased in a lead container, and it would remain behind a lead brick wall in the laboratory's fume hood during use until the residual solution, and any equipment which came in contact with it, were carefully disposed of as radioactive waste. By contrast, when I arrived for my treatment, I was asked to put my head into a fume hood and drink a tablespoon of water containing 100 mCi of radioactive iodine! This was counter to all of my previous 'radiation safety' training; however, I weighed my anxiety regarding the radiation against the benefit of preventing recurrence of my cancer, and drank the solution as directed. Then a technician stood 6 feet from me (we each held one end of the tape measure) and took a reading of my radiation output using a Geiger counter!

Because I had small children at home, I spent the next two nights in a hotel near my home. I had been told to keep an arm's distance from others for the first few days, so I drove through fast food restaurants and kept to myself. Most of the radioactivity is excreted in your urine during the first 48 hours, so I was careful to double flush the toilet in my hotel room. As any mother of young children, I had hoped that the silver lining of my imposed exile would be some pleasant quiet time to myself, but I was disappointed when the radioactivity affected my gastrointestinal system, and I experienced 2 days of low-grade nausea (akin to 'morning sickness').

I resumed taking my thyroid pills when I returned home. For the next week I slept alone (exposure is related to both distance and time of exposure), wore rubber gloves to prepare my children's food (because the radioactivity was present in my sweat; though I am sure this was overkill), ate off of paper plates with plastic utensils, and laundered my clothes separately. Overall, it was a very odd experience.

The final step in my initial treatment occurred 20 months after my treatment dose of radioactive iodine. I was placed on a low-iodine diet for 2 weeks and injected with Thyrogen (human recombinant TSH) to enhance uptake of the low-dose radioactive iodine into any residual thyroid cells. (The single intramuscular injection of Thyrogen was a far preferable way to increase TSH than a month off my thyroid pills!). As a veteran dieter, I found the low-iodine diet to be inconvenient, but not difficult. Primarily, I had to avoid salty foods (including processed meats and canned vegetables), seafood and dairy products. Immediately prior to the scan, I drank a low dose of radioactive iodine, then had to lie motionless on my back for approximately 30–60 minutes during the whole body scan. This was difficult for a borderline claustrophobic, as you are inside a (albeit open-ended) tube during the scan. I was relieved to learn that no residual thyroid cells were detected, and that my serum thyroglobulin levels were very low despite my increased TSH.

93. Following thyroidectomy for thyroid cancer, I am scheduled for I-131 scan and possible I-131. Why is this necessary?

Following thyroidectomy or near total thyroidectomy, I-131 scanning usually reveals residual activity in the operative site often called "the thyroid bed." I tell my patients this analogy. If I swept my exam room with a broom, I would get all the dust and dirt I could see. If I came back with a vacuum cleaner with a clean bag and vacuum-cleaned the room, I would find some dust and dirt in the clean bag that I had missed with the broom. The surgeon removed all the thyroid tissue apparent at the time of operation. If you use another means of finding thyroid tissue like I-131 scanning, then you usually detect residual thyroid tissue not seen by the surgeon. Taking a treatment dose of I-131 ablates any residual activity similar to using the vacuum cleaner. One reason to ablate any residual activity is that patients who receive I-131 have less frequency of recurrent tumors than those who do not receive I-131. Furthermore, if there is no thyroid tissue, serum thyroglobulin should be low (see Question 97). This aids follow-up in that a rising level of serum thyroglobulin indicates recurrence of the cancer. Finally, treating the thyroid remnant with I-131 allows for a post treatment scan (3–7 days later) which is helpful to determine if there is distal spread (metastasis) of cancer outside of the thyroid bed.

94. How much radiation will be administrated and how much radiation can I receive if further treatments are necessary?

Various centers use 30–100 mCi to treat remnant thyroid activity; the specific amount depends on the findings at surgery and institutional practices. Patients who are treated for thyroid cancer receive a dose of I-131, about 10-15 times that which is used for hyperthyroid patients. That's because thyroid cancer does not concentrate the I-131 as well as normal thyroid tissue (see Question 99). Most of the I-131 is excreted in the urine within the first 48 hours following treatment. Generally, nuclear medicine physicians avoid going over an accumulative I-131 dose of 800–1000 mCi to avoid the risk of bone marrow toxicity.

95. For how long does radioactive iodine remain in my body?

Radioactive iodine remains in your body for just a few days. Most of the radioactive iodine not retained in your thyroid is excreted in the urine within the first 48 hours after treatment. A small quantity will be present in the saliva, sweat and stools. The radioactive iodine that remains in your thyroid gland also decreases quickly. This means that the possibility of unnecessary radiation exposure to other people also decreases in a matter of days.

96. What precautions are necessary once I receive radioactive iodine?

Although generally safe for the treated patient, I-131 should be avoided by others as much as possible. Most of the damage to the thyroid occurs in the first few days after treatment. Since the half-life for I-131 is 8 days, there is a natural attrition of its radioactivity. In general, a distance of one arm's length should be maintained between the person treated and others who spend more than two hours next to the patient in any 24-hour period. This applies especially to children and pregnant women. While brief contact with a person after treatment is acceptable, sleeping together, watching television, going to movies, long car or plane trips should be avoided for approximately 7 days after the treatment. Since a small amount of radioactive iodine is found in saliva, one should not share food and utensils, including glasses, bottles, cans of soda, water, beer, etc. Dishes and eating utensils should be rinsed before being put with those of the rest of the family. Paper plates and plastic utensils should be used only if they are immediately disposed of outside the home. Cooking is fine, as long as the utensil used to taste the food while cooking is not re-used before rinsing. Keep your toothbrush separate from those belonging to the rest of your family. Again, much of the radioactive iodine, particularly in first few days post treatment, is excreted in the urine. The treated person should drink lots of liquids, especially water, and flush the toilet twice after using it. Be sure to thoroughly clean up any spilled urine. Laundry need not be washed separately unless the treated person has perspired profusely (such as after exercise), or has urinary incontinence. It is extremely important that women who are breast-feeding stop before the radioactive agent is given, because iodine is concentrated and excreted in breast milk. Pregnancy should be avoided for six months following treatment. All of this can be summed up in three principles: distance (radiation decreases significantly as the distance from you increases); time (only brief exposure of others to you); and hygiene (good hygiene minimizes the possibilities of direct contamination with radioactive iodine).

97. Following surgery and radioactive I-131 treatment for papillary thyroid cancer, my endocrinologist ordered a serum thyroglobulin. What is serum thyroglobulin?

Thyroglobulin, a large protein produced only in thyroid tissue, binds both T4 and T3 within the thyroid follicule (see Question 1). A small amount of this protein escapes into the bloodstream so it can be assayed in the serum. Normal thyroid tissue, benign nodular disease, and well-differentiated thyroid carcinomas make thyroglobulin. Serum thyroglobulin determinations cannot distinguish between benign or malignant thyroid nodules. Once all normal and diseased thyroid tissue is removed via surgery and radio-iodine ablation, serum thyroglobulin levels are very low or non-measurable. Thyroglobulin levels are quite helpful in follow-up of well-differentiated thyroid carcinoma. The serum thyroglobulin should be low in patients who have no thyroid tissue. An elevated thyroglobulin level several weeks after surgery and ablative remnant treatment indicates persistent disease somewhere in the body. Serum thyroglobulin circulates for several weeks following ablation because of its prolonged half-life. Thyroid cancer cells respond to TSH stimulation and produce thyroglobulin. One may raise TSH levels by stopping levothyroxine (producing hypothyroidism) or administering human recombinant TSH (Thyrogen) intramuscularly and measuring "stimulated" thyroglobulin. This is a much more sensitive method of detecting recurrent well-differentiated thyroid cancer than measuring baseline serum thyroglobulin while on thyroid suppressive therapy. If the baseline serum thyroglobulin is elevated, then no TSH stimulation is necessary. The "stimulated" thyroglobulin is helpful to detect recurrent/ persistent thyroid cancer only if serum thyroglobulin levels are low. The major drawback of current serum thyroglobulin assays is that if there are circulating antibodies to thyroglobulin (as there are in up to 30% of patients with thyroid cancer), then serum thyroglobulin determinations are useless and totally without merit in following such patients. A few patients with thyroid cancer lose these anti-thyroglobulin antibodies with time and then the serum thyroglobulin becomes helpful.

98. Mrs. Lobaugh, what has been your experience dealing with thyroid cancer?

Mrs. Lobaugh's comments:

After the initial shock of the diagnosis, I have considered myself blessed to have what is certainly a treatable, if not curable, disease. Although no one chooses to have surgery, after the initial thyroidectomy and treatment, this disease has had very little effect on my life. I take a daily pill, as do many people, and I see my endocrinologist annually for monitoring, as is prudent.

99. Why is a low-iodine diet used in preparation for a body scan?

Thyroid tissues, both normal and abnormal, trap iodine. The normal thyroid literally gobbles up any circulating iodine. Thyroid cancer cells are very much less efficient in trapping iodine; that is, such cells have a low avidity for iodine. Once normal thyroid tissue is removed by surgery and previous radioactive iodine ablation, then the abnormal (thyroid cancer) cells may trap or concentrate iodine. These cells cannot tell the difference between radioactive ("hot") iodine and non-radioactive ("cold") iodine. They trap iodine ("hot" or "cold") with equal avidity. If many "cold" iodine molecules are circulating and you take a small dose of "hot" iodine, the number of "hot" molecules taken up by tissue will be low because both the "cold" and "hot" iodine compete for entrance into these cells. The sheer number of "cold" iodine molecules trapped overrides the "hot" iodine molecules trapped, leading to less uptake of radioactive iodine. Since the imaging studies look for "hot" iodine, very little to nothing will be seen when there is plenty of "cold" iodine circulating. By lessening the amount of "cold" iodine, you enhance the possibility for thyroid tissue to concentrate "hot" iodine. This is where the low iodine (which is "cold") comes. The majority of iodine one ingests is excreted in the urine. After a few days on a low iodine diet, the pool of "cold" iodine is much lower. This facilitates the uptake of "hot" iodine used to scan for thyroid tissue. **Table 10** outlines foods that should be avoided and those which are permitted. In addition, all vitamins with iodine should be avoided (if you are unsure, don't take them). You should start this regimen (dietary restriction of iodine and no iodine-containing preparations such as kelp, seaweed, etc.) two weeks prior to scanning.

Table 10 Low-Iodine Diet

AVOID
Iodized salt and sea salt
All dairy products (milk, sour cream, cheese, cream, yogurt, butter, ice cream, eggnog)
Margarine
Egg yolks
Seafood (fish, shellfish, seaweed, kelp)
Foods made with seaweed (carrageen, agar-agar, algin, alginate)
Cured and corned foods (ham, hotdogs, bacon, sausage, corned beef, tuna, luncheon meat, etc.)
Marinated chicken or turkey
Dried fruit and potato skins
Canned foods (vegetables including sauerkraut, soups, sauces, meats)
Bread products (most commercial breads contain iodate, pancakes and muffin mixes)
Chocolate
Molasses
Soy products (soy sauce, soy milk, tofu)
EAT
Fresh chicken, turkey, and beet in moderate amounts
Black pepper and fresh or dried herbs for seasoning
Homemade bread made with non-iodized salt and oil (not soy) instead of butter or milk
Most fresh fruits and vegetables (washed well)
Frozen vegetables and fruits that have no added salt
Canned peaches, pears, and pineapples
Unsalted nuts
Unsalted Matzo crackers and unsalted rice cakes
Clear sodas
Coffee or tea made from distilled water (use just a little of non-dairy creamer—no cream)
Popcorn popped in vegetable oil or air popped with non-iodized salt

100. After surgery to remove a thyroid nodule, the final pathology was reported as medullary thyroid carcinoma. How is this cancer different from other thyroid cancers?

The thyroid contains two types of cells: follicular cells and parafollicular cells. These cells differ in origin and function. The thyroid follicular cells develop from the floor of the mouth, whereas the parafollicular cells migrate into the developing thyroid gland from the embryonic neural crest. This difference in cell origin helps explain the many different clinical presentations noted. Follicular cells make thyroid hormone and parafollicular cells, or "C" cells, produce calcitonin. Well-differentiated thyroid cancers (papillary/follicular) originate from follicular cells, and **medullary thyroid carcinoma** (MTC) originate from parafollicular cells. About 5% of all thyroid carcinomas are of the MTC variety. Regardless of origin, both types of carcinoma require surgery as the primary therapy. Although I-131 ablation and thyroid suppression are necessary adjuvant therapies for the follicular cell variants of thyroid carcinoma, these forms of treatment do not work for MTC because "C" cells do not concentrate iodine and are not stimulated by TSH. Extensive neck surgery to remove the thyroid and any lymph nodes is the treatment for MTC. Of course, following thyroidectomy, thyroxine replacement is necessary for MTC patients as well. Because MTCs make calcitonin, physicians use serum calcitonin levels to follow the course and activity of this disease post-operatively. Clinically, MTC may be divided in to two types: sporadic and familial. Sporadic MTC usually presents as a single nodule in older individuals (> 40 years). The cancer is isolated to one lobe of the thyroid, although there may be regional

Medullary thyroid carcinoma

A form of cancer that has its origin in the farafollicular, or "C" cells, of the thyroid.

metastasis. There is no family history of MTC. Familial MTC, as the name states, is hereditary. Familial MTC patients present much earlier in life than those with sporadic MTC. By the time of presentation, patients with familial MTC have tumor involving both thyroid lobes. Prior to development of overt familial MTC cancer, an incubation period earmarked by "C" cell **hyperplasia** and elevated calcitonin levels occurs. The gene for MTC is well described. Genetic testing identifies individuals within a family who carry the gene. Prophylactic thyroidectomy prevents MTC in these affective individuals. Since neural crest tissue is involved in the development of MTC, patients with familial MTC often experience involvement of other tissues (multiple endocrine neoplasia—MEN). These tissues include the parathyroid glands (elevated serum calcium), gastric secretory tumors (gastrinomas), skin tumors (neurofibromas), and adrenal tumors (pheochromocytomas). Skin and mucosa tumors (really neurofibromas) form visible markers of familial MTC. The left panel of **Figure 26** demonstrates a mucosa neuroma on the tongue of a five-year-old girl who already had MTC at surgery; while the right panel shows similar lesions on the tongue of her mother who died a couple years after receiving the diagnosis of MTC. Familial

Hyperplasia

Increased number of "C" cells.

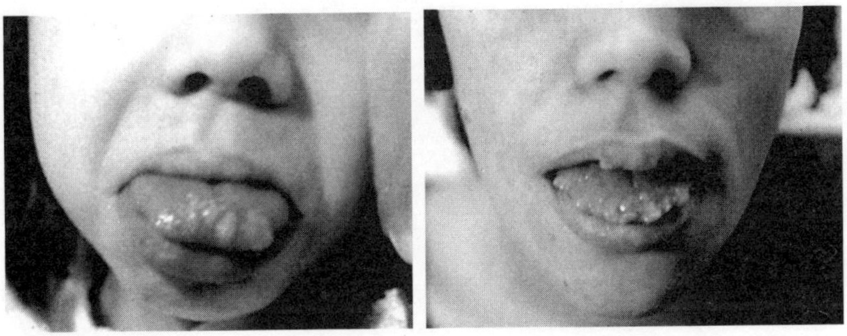

Figure 26 The mucosal neuromas of familial MTC (type IIB).
Child with mucosal neuroma on the tongue (left panel) and her mother's tongue (right panel). These were the only visible findings in this serious condition.

MTC may be characterized by quite aggressive tumors associated with a life expectancy of only a few years. Finally, MTC differs from anaplastic thyroid carcinoma, a virulent, progressive cancer of undifferentiated thyroid cells that causes death literally in months. Fortunately, this type of cancer is uncommon. Surgery rarely cures this tumor and there is no proven chemotherapy for anaplastic thyroid carcinoma.

Resources

American Association of Clinical Endocrinologists
Suite 205
1000 Riverside Avenue
Jacksonville, Florida 32204
904-353-7878
Website: *www.aace.com*

American Cancer Society
Phone: 800-ACS-2345 (800-227-2345)
Website: *www.cancer.org*

American Thyroid Association
Suite 650
6066 Leesburg Pike
Falls Church, Virginia 22041
703-998-8890
Website: *www.thyroid.org*

British Thyroid Foundation
Post Office Box 97
Clifford, Wetherby
West Yorkshire, LS23 6XD
Tel: +44 (0) 1423 709707
Fax: +44 (0) 1423 709448
Website: *www.btf-thyroid.org*

The Endocrine Society
Suite 900
8401 Connecticut Avenue
Chevy Chase, Maryland 20815
301-941-0200
Website: *www.endo-society.org*

Genzyme Corporation
500 Kendall Street
Cambridge, Massachusetts 02142
Phone: 1-888-799-3884
Website: *www.thyrogen.com*

National Cancer Institute
31 Center Drive, MSC 2580
Bethesda, Maryland 20892-2580
Phone: 800-4-Cancer (800-422-6237)
Website: *www.nci.nih.gov*

National Graves' Disease Foundation (USA)
Post Office Box 8387
Fleming Island, Florida 32006
Tel/fax: 904-278-9488
Website: *www.ngdf.org*

Thyroid Foundation of America
One Longfellow Place, Suite 1518
Boston, Massachusetts 02114
Tel: 800-832-8321
Fax: 617-534-1515
Website: *www.allthyroid.org*

ThyCa: The Thyroid Cancer
Survivors' Association
Post Office Box 1545
New York, New York 10159-1545
Phone: 1-877-588-7904 (toll free)
E-mail: thyca@thyca.org
Website: *www.thyca.org*

Glossary

A

Agranulocytosis: a rare allergic reaction (due to long-term use of Methimazole) in which while blood counts lead to infection, sore throat, mouth ulcer, fever, and possible death.

Amyloidosis: abnormal deposits of amyloid protein in many tissues including the thyroid.

Anaplastic: aggressive cancer cells that lose the distinguishing characteristic of the original tissue.

Antithyroid medication: drugs that block thyroid hormone production, such as methimazole or propylthiouracil (PTU).

B

Benign: not cancerous.

Blepharoplasty: a functional or cosmetic surgical procedure intended to reshape the upper eyelid or lower eyelid by the removal and/or repositioning of excess tissue as well as by reinforcement of surrounding muscles and tendons.

Biopsy: a procedure in which cells are collected for microscopic examination.

C

Calcifications: tiny mineral deposits in thyroid tissue that may or may not represent cancerous tissue.

Calcitonin: a protein made by the parafollicular or "C" cells of the thyroid; high levels are a marker of medullary thyroid carcinoma.

Cancer: a malignancy that can have several origins.

Carcinoma: another word for cancer.

Cardioversion: electrical shock across the chest wall to reset the heart rate to normal sinus rhthym.

Cells: basic elements of tissue; each cell is unique to the tissue of which it is a part.

Conjunctiva: transparent skin over the front ofthe eye.

Cyst: a fluid-sac that feels like a lump; a cyst may or may not be able to be felt depending on its size and location; cysts are usually benign.

Cytopathologist: a doctor specifically trained to look at small amounts of tissue to determine what type of tissue is being examined.

D

Diplopoa: commonly known as double vision; the simultaneous perception of two images of a single object.

E

Endocrine: dealing glandular secretion of hormones.

Endocrinologist: a physician who specializes in the diagnosis and treatment of endocrine disorders.

Endogenous: the thyroid itself releasing more thyroid.

Euthyroidism: normal thyroid levels.

F

Familial: hereditary; processes that cluster or run in families.

Fine needle aspiration biopsy: using a thin needle to collect fluid or cells directly from a mass or nodule for microscopic evaluation.

G

Goiter: an enlarged and usually visible thyroid gland presenting as fullness in the anterior lower neck.

Graves' disease: an autoimmune condition in which increased levels of thyroid cause hyperthyroidism, which may also present with prominent and protruding eyes and changes over lower legs and feet called pretibial myxedema.

H

Hashimoto's thyroiditis: an autoimmune state in which the thyroid is destroyed, causing hypothyroidism and often a goiter.

Hematoma: blood clot.

Hormones: chemicals that are made by glands and released into the circulation, they travel to specific target organs to affect processes; for example, thyroid stimulating hormone is produced by the pituitary and circulates to the thyroid, where the thyroid makes thyroxine.

Hyperplasia: increased number of cells.

Hyperthyroidism: condition in which too much thyroid hormone circulates, causing a variety of symptoms including increased nervousness, agitation, heart rate, etc.; also thyrotoxicosis or overactive thyroid.

Hypocalcemia: a condition that might follow thyroid surgery if parathyroid function is compromised.

Hypothyroidism: a condition in which less than normal thyroid hormone circulates, causing decreases in metabolic activity that presents in a variety of symptoms including fatigue, depression, cold intolerance, etc.; also known as underactive thyroid.

I

Iodine: the naturally occurring element (molecular weight 127) necessary for thyroid hormone production.

Isotope: one or more atoms having same atomic number (protons) but different molecular weights (neurons).

I-131: the radioactive isotope of iodine that emits radiation used to treat hyperthyroidism and well-differentiated thyroid carcinoma.

L

Lagophthalmos: the inability to close the eyelids completely.

M

Malignant: cancerous; which may grow rapidly and out of control.

Medullary thyroid carcinoma: a form of cancer that has its origin in the parafollicular or "C" cells of the thyroid.

Metabolism: the process of the sum total of chemical reactions necessary for living things.

Metastasis, metastasize: spread of cancer.

Myxedema: Physical features due to lack of thyroid hormone causing puffy eyelids, facial edema, and fluid retention.

N

Nodule: a lump or clump of tissue that forms a mass that may or may not be palpable.

O

Osteoporosis: loss of bone mineral and bone integrity that may lead to fracture.

P

Palpable, palpation: something that can be felt with the fingertips or the process thereof.

Papillary thyroid carcinoma: the most common cause of thyroid cancer, distinguished by its microscopic features.

Parathyroid glands: glands located adjacent to the thyroid that control calcium levels in the blood.

Pertechnetate: a compound containing the TcO_4^- compound.

Pituitary: the master gland located between and behind the eyes that controls the adrenal, thyroid, and sex glands.

Post-partum thyroiditis: an inflammation of the thyroid following pregnancy that often has three stages (hyperthyroidism, euthyroid, then hypothyroidism); usually transient and without permanent complications.

Proptosis, exophthalmos: the forward movement of the eyeball or bulging eyes.

S

Subacute thyroiditis: often a painless inflammatory condition leading to transient hyperthyroidism.

T

Thyroidectomy: surgical removal of all (total) or part (subtotal) of the thyroid; removal of either lobe of the thyroid is called lobectomy.

Thyroid: the glandular structure in the lower neck that makes thyroxine; also, the chemical, thyroxine, may be referred to as thyroid.

Thyroid nodule: a lump, bump, or mass in the thyroid that may be large enough to feel (palpated) or too small to be felt and only seen with ultrasound; the nodule may be benign or malignant.

Thyroid radioactive uptake, thyroid uptake: a measure of thyroid function using a counter that detects radioactive iodine activity following administration of an isotope; for example, a normal thyroid uptake of iodine would be 10–30% of the dose administered 24 hours earlier.

Thyroid scan: an imaging study using radioactive isotopes to visualize the thyroid gland.

Thyroglobulin: a large protein made only by the thyroid, but which should not be present after the thyroid is missing; used as a marker for persistent or recurrent thyroid carcinoma.

Thyroiditis: an inflammation of the thyroid that may or may not be tender. In the early and acute stages it presents as hyperthyroidism; in the latter or chronic stage with hypothyroidism.

Thyromegaly: Tyromegaly is interchangeable with "goiter."

Thyrotoxic: Thyrotoxic symptoms are hyperthyroid symptoms and can encompass a wide range of manifestations. Hyperthyroidism and thyrotoxicosis are often used interchangeably.

Thyrotroph: the pituitary cells that produce TSH.

Thyrotropin: Thyroid stimulating hormone (TSH); a chemical made by the pituitary that causes thyroid hormone secretion.

Thyroxine: chemical made by the thyroid containing four iodine molecules; also called thyroid, L-thyroxine, levothyroxine, or T4.

Total body scan: Using I-131 to determine whether any residual thyroid tissue remains following surgery to remove the thyroid; used mainly in follow-up of thyroid cancer.

Triiodothyronine: an active form of thyroid hormone that contains three iodine molecules instead of four, as in thyroxine; also called T3.

U

Ultrasound, ultrasonography: a means to identify anatomy of an organ using ultrasound techniques; a valuable aid to follow size but not function of a structure such as a thyroid nodule.

Index

Note: A *t* following a page number indicates a table; an italic page number indicates a figure.

A

B

C

D

E

F

G

H

I

L

M

N

O

P

U

V

W

Notes